PLASTICS
FOR MODELLERS

PLASTICS
FOR MODELLERS

Alex Weiss

Cartoons by Bob Graham

Nexus Special Interests

This book is for Tom, who should understand the meaning of most of the lengthy names which occur in the text.

Nexus Special Interests Ltd.
Nexus House
Azalea Drive
Swanley
Kent, BR8 8HU

First published 1998

© 1998 Alex Weiss

ISBN 1-85486-170-0

Printed and bound in Great Britain by Biddles Ltd., Guildford and King's Lynn

Contents

Acknowledgements	x

Introduction	xi
The strengths, weaknesses and uses of plastics in modelling	xii
Plastic additives	xiv
Plastics derived from nature	xvi
Amber	xvi
Bitumen	xvi
Casein	xvi
Natural rubber	xvi
Shellac	xvi

Part 1 – Types of plastic materials	1

Chapter 1 Thermoplastics and thermosetting plastics	2
Thermoplastics	2
ABS (acrylonitrile butadiene styrene)	2
Acetal (polyacetal)	2
Delrin	3
Duracon	3
Acrylic (polymethyl methacrylate)	3
Perspex	4
Cellulose plastics (celluloid)	4
Cellulose acetate (acetate)	4
Cellulose acetate butyrate (butyrate)	4
Cellulose nitrate	4
Polyamides	4
Nylon	4
Nylon 66	5
Glass-filled nylon 66	5
Cast nylon 6	5
MoS^2 filled cast nylon 6	5
Nylatron GS	5
Nyloil	5
Kevlar	5
Torlon	6
Bearing grade	6
Electrical grade	6
Tufnol	6
Carp brand	6

Kite brand	6
Whale brand	6
10G/40	6
Polycarbonate	6
Corotherm	7
Corex	7
Lexan	7
Polyester	7
Mylar and melinex	7
Polyethylene (polythene)	8
Polypropylene	8
Polystyrene (styrene)	8
Evergreen, Plastruct and Plasticard	8
Expanded polystyrene	9
PTFE (polytetrafluoroethylene) also called teflon or fluon	9
Viton	9
PVA (polyvinyl acetate)	9
PVC (polyvinyl chloride)	10
Fablon	10
Thermosetting plastics	10
Acrylic	11
Epoxy	11
Phenolic	12
Bakelite	12
Phenolic laminates	12
Formica	12
Formaldehydes (aminos)	12
MF (melamine formaldehyde)	13
UF (urea formaldehyde)	13
Polyester	14
Isopon	14
Victrex	14
Polyurethane	14
Tufset	15
Silicone	15
Silicone rubber	15
RTV-11	15
RTV-31	15
RTV-420	15
RTV-428	15
Catalysts for silicone rubber	15

Tixo TA1 thixotropic additive	16
Cab-O-Sil	16
Maestro acrylic/PVA polymers	16
DP100	16
Silicone fluid	16
SF-96-50 silicone fluid	16
Synthetic rubber (diene and olefin rubbers)	16
SBR (styrene-butadiene rubber)	16
NBR (nitrile rubber)	16
Klingersil	16
CR (chloroprene rubber)	16
Neoprene	17

Chapter 2 Basic forms of plastics   18

Identification of plastics	18
Visual and mechanical testing	18
Flame testing	19
Synthetic rubbers	20
Solvent tests	20
Material selection	21
Available shapes and sizes	22
Sheet	22
Foam board	24
Paxolin and GRP sheet	24
Acrylic products	24
Transparent coloured sheeting	24
Extrusions	24
Plastic sections	25
ABS	25
Stryrene products	25
Plasticard sheet	25
Plasticard strip	26
Plasticard micro rod	26
Other forms	26
Belts	26
Box strapping	26
Cable ties	26
Fillers	26
Foams	27
Grommets	27
Lubricants	27
Silicone- and teflon-based oils	27
Moulded carvings	27
Nylon nuts and bolts	27
Pipes and tubing	27

Sealants and gasket materials	28
Hematite	28
Pipe-jointing compounds	28
Silicone rubber	28
Epoxy putties	28
Potting compounds	28
Epoxy	28
Polyurethane	28
Silicone rubber	28
Fabrics, cords and threads	28
Where to get them	29
Yellow Pages	29
Specialist suppliers	30
Model shops	30
DIY stores	30
Mail order	30
Scrap and scrap yards	30
Modifying household items	31
Plastics as a storage medium	31
Bags	31
Boxes, drawers and racks	31
Covers	31
Protection	31

Part 2 – Working with plastics   32

Health and safety	32
Working with GRP and silicone rubber	32
Storage of plastics	33
Disposal	33

Chapter 3 Working plastics with hand and power tools   34

Hand working plastics	34
Bending	34
Cutting	34
Knives	34
Scissors	35
Saws and nibblers	35
Removing material	35
Sanding	35
Filing	35
Scraping	36
Planing	36
Polishing	36
Drilling and thread cutting	36

Using power tools 36
  Cutting 37
    Band saws 37
    Circular saws 37
    Jig saws 37
    Laminate trimmers 37
  Drilling 37
  Turning 38
    Tools 38
  Milling and routing 38
  Sanding 39
  Polishing 39
Finishing models 39
  Etchants 39
  Solvents 39
    Acetone 39
    Cellulose thinners 39
  Cleaners 40
Anti-static 40
  Tack cloths 40
Dopes, paints and varnishes 40
  Acrylics 40
  Celluloses 41
  Enamels 41
  Epoxies 41
  Polyurethanes 41
Self-adhesive sheeting and strips 41
  Decals 42
  Lettering 42
Dyeing 42

Chapter 4 Joining plastics to themselves and other materials 43
The choice of adhesives 43
  Acrylic 44
  Aliphatic 46
  Anaerobic 46
  Cement 46
  Contact glue 47
  Cyano 47
  Epoxy 47
  Hot glue 48
  Polyester 48
  PVA 48
  Urea formaldehyde 49
General-purpose and specialist glues 49

Aerosol spray cans of fixing glues 49
Welding plastics with heat or solvents 49
  Chloroform 49
  Methyl ethyl ketone (MEK) 50
  Micro Weld, Plastic Magic and
    Plastic Weld 50
Tapes 50
  Insulating tape 50
  Self-amalgamating tape 50
  Double-sided tape 50
  Foam tape 50
  Thread-sealing tape 50
  Packing tape 50
  Velcro tape 50

Chapter 5 Heat forming and vacuum forming 51
Using heat 51
  Cooling 52
  Bending 53
  Heat sealing cord and thread 53
Heat forming 53
Vacuum forming 53
  Equipment 54
  Forms 54
  Forming 54
Casting 55
Heat joining 55
Hot glue 56
Heat-shrink covering materials 55
  Heat-shrink sleeving 56

Chapter 6 Rubber moulds and components 57
Silicone rubber 57
  Storage, handling and mixing 57
  Thickening, thinning and colouring 58
  Release agents 58
  Making a mould 58
    Single-piece moulds 59
    Two-piece moulds 59
    Strip-off skin moulds 60
Items from silicone rubber 60
Encapsulation 62
Hot-melt vinyl 62
Latex 62

Chapter 7 Composite materials and resin casting 64

Glass reinforced plastic 64
Designing the moulding and mould 65
  Designing in strength 66
  Moulding thickness 66
  Weight 66
  Strength 66
Resins 67
  Polyester resin 67
  Epoxy resin 67
  Acrylic resin 67
Additives 68
  Colloidal silica 68
  Micro-fibres 68
  Micro-balloons 68
  Metal and stone powders 68
Carbon fibre and kevlar 68
Making the mould 69
Fabrication methods 69
  The moulding 70
Repairs 70
Resin casting 70
  Clear casting 71
  Epoxy castings 72
  Polyurethane resin castings 72
Coatings 72

Chapter 8 Expanded polystyrene and other foams 73

Rigid foam 73
  Cutting 75
  Shaping 77
  Adhesives 77
Polyurethane foam 77
Soft foams 78

Chapter 9 Plastic kits and styrene 79

Plastic kits 79
  Assembly 81
  Customised parts 81
Styrene materials 82
  Cutting sheet 83
  Cutting strips 83
Joining parts 83
  Adhesives 84

Styrene to styrene 84
Styrene to metal or wood 85
Painting and decoration 85

Part 3 – Applications of plastics 86

Chapter 10 Flying models 87

Model aircraft 87
  Plastic models 89
  Ancillary items 89
  Covering materials 91
    Nylon 91
    Films 92
    Textured coverings 92
  Decoration 93
  Foam components 93
  Wings 93
  Composite components 93
  Ducted fans and turbojets 94
Radio controlled helicopters 94
Model rockets 95
  Parachutes 95
Balloons and airships 95
Kites 96

Chapter 11 Ships and boats 97

Model boats 97
  Hulls and fittings 97
  Yacht sails 99
    Laminated sails 99
  Rigging 100
  Superstructure 100
  Fittings and decoration 100
  Radio control 100
  Waterproof seals 101
  Submarines 101
Hovercraft 102

Chapter 12 Cars and land vehicles 103

Model cars 103
  R/C cars 103
    Chassis items 104
    Tyres and tracks 105
  Freelance working models 106
  Electric slot cars 106
Motorcycles 107

Trams 107
Carriages, caravans and carts 108

Chapter 13 Buildings and layouts 109
Buildings 109
Working styrene 110
  Surface finish 110
  Windows and door holes 110
  Roofs 110
Dolls' houses 111
Layouts 113
  Scatter materials 114
  Water 115
  Trees and plants 115
Model railways 116
  Locomotives and rolling stock 117
    Rivets 117
  Track and track bed 118
  Line-side accessories 118
Wargaming 118
Military modelling 119
Dioramas 119

Chapter 14 Figures 121
Aircraft pilots and crew 121
Animals 122
Boat crew 122
Dolls and puppets 123
Figures for vehicles and trains 124
Military modelling 125
Wargaming figures 126
Converting figures 127

Chapter 15 Model engineering 128
Bearings 128
Belt drives 128
  Toothed belts 129
  Poly-V belts, round belts and
    V or wedge belts 129
  Twist-link belting 129
Diaphragms 130

Electroplating 130
Flexible pipes 130
Friction rollers 130
Gears 130
Heat-insulation materials 131
Seals and O-rings 131
Shims 131
Shock and vibration mounts 131
Tippex 132
Tufnol leaf springs 132
Applications 132
  Clocks 132
  Internal-combustion engines 133
  Model guns 133
  Machine and other workshop
    tools 134
  Scientific instruments 134
  Steam-powered models 134
  Other vehicles 135
  Hot-air engines 135
Plastic engineering 135

Chapter 16 Electrical and electronics 137
Capacitors 138
Conduit and trunking 138
Containers and housings 138
Insulators and seals 138
Heat-shrink tube 138
Heat-sink compounds 139
Nuts, bolts and spacers 139
PCBs (printed circuit boards) 139
Wiring 140
Potting 140
Robotics 141

Appendix A Bibliography and list of useful addresses 142
Bibliography 142
List of useful addresses 143

Index of plastics 144

Acknowledgements

Many people in the industry which supports modellers have contributed both information and photographs that appear in this book. It is only their support which has made this volume possible.

Chapters 6 and 7, dealing with silicone rubber and composite materials have relied heavily on the information provided by John Tiranti, managing director of Alec Tiranti Ltd. He generously provided me with photographic illustrations on computer disk and two booklets, **The Silicon Rubber Booklet** and **The Polyester Resin Booklet**. Scott Bader, the owners of Strand, have also allowed me to use the illustrations from their pamphlet **A Guide to Glassfibre** for which I am most grateful.

I was greatly helped by John Bristow of Deluxe Materials (Models) who provided both photographs and copies of informative articles dealing with adhesives. He also commented on my draft

Alex Weiss sticking a machine gun, made from a plastic hair curler, to the cowl of his Fokker D8.

of Chapter 4 and helped with some constructive criticism.

Joanne Cassidy of the Dolls' House Emporium kindly loaned me several illustrations used in Chapter 13, while Mr C.M. Pritchard of Pritchard Patent Product Co Ltd, better known as Peco, provided a range of model railway illustrations. Fredrik Jacobsson took time to send me a picture of the Maxicraft Hot Wire Cutter.

Brian L. Ellerby, president of Evergreen Scale Models went to a great deal of effort to send me both photographs and information from the USA about the company's range of products, which are reflected in Chapter 9.

A number of Nexus Special Interest books have provided a very useful source of information, including **Radio Control Model Yachts** by Trevor Reece and **The Car Modeller's Handbook** by Mat Irvine. Beverly Laughlin of Nexus Special Interests provided me with copies of a number of useful specialist magazines produced by the company.

Cedric Verdon supplied much information and several photographs of models made in casting resin. These are shown in Chapters 6 and 7, which he read and commented on constructively.

I should also mention Claude Smale, whose book on creative plastic techniques and enthusiasm encouraged me to start writing this volume. I also much appreciate the forbearance of my wife for living with my obsession for putting this book together.

Finally, I recognise that many names of commercial plastics are registered trademarks but, for simplicity, I have rarely used a capital letter for their names and I have not included the ® symbol after their names each time they appear in the text.

Introduction

For most people, plastic modelling means assembling kits of aircraft, boats, figures, land vehicles or spacecraft. For a few, it means constructing buildings from the wide range of styrene sheet, strip and extrusions sold in most model shops.

Purist woodworkers, and metal workers for that matter, usually shudder at the mention of plastics. The word has historic implications of cheap and nasty. This is hardly fair as there are few woodworkers who never use PVA white woodworkers' glue or polyurethane varnish, or even shellac; all of them plastics. Those who work metals generally swear by Loctite products, again plastics, and drive their lathes and accessories with plastic drive belts. This prejudice is, perhaps, the result of stories about some of the early applications of plastics which have become myths as materials technology in this area has improved.

So what are plastics? Well might you enquire. To give a clear concise answer is not easy. I consider that plastics are man-made materials which can be produced in a required form or shaped by chemical reaction or the application of heat and/or pressure. The popular ones today depend on their physical and chemical properties, allied to their cost. It is worth remembering that a plastic may quickly become obsolete if a new one comes on the market which is cheaper or has much improved properties.

You might ask why anyone would wish to write a book about plastics. Well, as a modeller for many years, I have built free-flight and radio controlled model aircraft, model boats, submarines, yachts and electric slot cars, not to mention OO and N gauge railways, a puppet theatre and a dolls' house, as well as enjoying military modelling and war games. I have found an increasing need to use plastics in these hobbies. In addition I own a well-equipped workshop with lathe and milling machine and have built steam models and workshop tools. I have also built my own radio control system and developed a number of electronic circuits for my models.

In all these endeavours, despite a preference to work with wood or metal, I have found I needed

Figure 1 The tap, in mid air, pours water down a clear plastic pipe up which the water is pumped.

to make plenty of use of plastic materials. Indeed, there are many jobs today which are really only practical using a suitable plastic. The problem which often arises is, which material is the right one and how can I work with it to get the best results? Unfortunately, I found that apart from books on R/C foam modelling, working with glass fibre and adhesives, there was little available in the way of written material on the subject of plastics for the average modeller.

This book divides into three main parts. It starts by describing the types of plastic available. It then examines the various ways of working with plastics, from using basic hand tools and turning them in a lathe through to building and modifying plastic kits. Finally, it considers the applications of these materials to the various different branches of modelling. These include all types of flying models, boats and road vehicles, layouts and buildings for model railways, military modelling and war games, not forgetting dolls' houses. It

Figure 2 A typical selection of plastics found in the home from pens, boxes and bottles to CDs.

also covers model figures, model engineering, and finally electrical and electronic construction. This book does not aim to tell you how to build all these models, but does attempt to show you where you can use plastics in their construction and how to work these plastic materials.

Plastics are very widely used in our society today. Everything from car interiors and bumpers to computer cases, from ball point pens to the clothes we wear benefit from the judicious use of plastics. Many of you may have some sense of aesthetic dislike of plastics, the very word sending a shiver through some. However, many modern plastics are much more like natural materials than in the past and a lot of them allow you to achieve results which are unobtainable with natural materials.

It is hard to imagine some areas of modelling without plastics. 'Airfix' kits and plastic figures, plastic paints, adhesives and covering materials, GRP and ABS mouldings, acetate glazing sheets … the list is endless. Some are used as a replacement for traditional materials such as wood, glass and metal. Others have found applications in their own right, particularly in terms of affordability.

The strengths, weaknesses and uses of plastics in modelling

One of the earliest recorded plastics is amber, a fossilised piece of which was supposed to contain the dinosaur DNA used to create *Jurassic Park*. There are a few other plastics which occur in nature, such as horn, rubber, gutta percha and shellac, but this book is aimed at exploring the uses of man-made plastics. The earliest of these date back to the 1860s and the majority have been produced since the 1930s as the petroleum industry has rapidly expanded. It was the shortage of natural materials such as rubber, during the Second World War, which forced the development of plastics apace. Almost all plastics today are the by-products of the fossil fuels, oil and coal, though a few are still processed from plants and even from milk!

There are many industrial processes used in the manufacture of items from plastic, such as

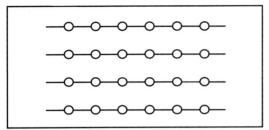

Figure 3 *Thermoplastics consist of long chains of molecules making them easy to form.*

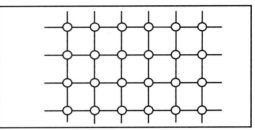

Figure 4 *The rigidity of thermosetting plastics comes from the cross-links between their chains of molecules.*

extrusion, blow, compression, injection and rotation moulding, lamination and coating which are of little practical use to the average modeller. On the other hand, heat treatment, vacuum forming, composite fabrication and working with foams and expanded plastics as well as cutting, filing and machining plastics are practical for the average modeller.

Plastics are excellent insulators which often results in a build up of static electrical charge. This can cause inconvenience when preparing plastics for painting or keeping transparent surfaces clean and dust free. Modern additives have significantly reduced this problem which can also destroy some electronic components.

Without going into the chemistry of plastics, it is useful to understand that plastics are made

from long-chain molecules called polymers. In thermoplastics, these are free to slide past each other as shown in Figure 3. Thermosetting plastics, on the other hand, are shown in Figure 4 and have links between the chains. They cannot be reheated and reshaped once they have been formed by the initial use of heat or chemical reaction during the manufacturing process. You should be aware that some plastics do not strictly lie in either of these two categories.

Thus it is clear that there is a group of plastics which can be softened and reshaped many times by the application of a moderate amount of heat – the thermoplastics. A typical example is acetate sheet. The second group – the thermosetting materials – are permanently rigid and you cannot

'I'M MAKING LONG CHAIN MOLECULES'

reshape them. A typical example is epoxy glue. More than one plastic may be mixed together or alloyed during manufacture to enhance particular properties. ABS is an alloy of acrylonitrile, butadiene and styrene.

Plastic additives

Most polymers have additives introduced during the process of manufacturing the final material to improve their qualities in some way. There are plasticisers that soften plastics which are basically hard. PVC pipes are hard while PVC sheeting is flexible, though both are made from the same basic plastic. Lubricants similarly make some plastics flow more easily during manufacture. Catalysts speed up chemical reactions when materials are undergoing change and their use in hardening glass fibre resin is a typical example. Pigments are used to self-colour plastics while fillers can improve impact or heat resistance. Stabilisers and anti-oxidants help plastics to survive in the natural environment longer, particularly resisting the sun's ultra-violet rays. This is good for our purposes but far from ideal in terms of biodegradability in the environment. Finally, solvents weaken thermoplastics in a similar way to heat and are used both for cleaning these materials and for welding them together.

Thermoplastics have two properties which are important in terms of their reaction to heat. First, their thermal conductivity is low, making them good insulators but making it difficult to heat a sheet of thermoplastic to an even temperature throughout. Their second property is that they have a large heat capacity, which also means they retain their heat well once hot. In terms of insulation, plastics are four to eight times worse than wood but hundreds to thousands of times better than metals like steel and copper. Plastics also expand when heated, and contract when cooled, much more than metals; up to eight times as much for some materials.

Thermoplastics can stretch and revert to their original size when the force is released, providing you do not exceed their elastic limit. None is as stretchy as rubber and, of course, the thermosetting plastics are hard and rigid. All plastics tend to become more brittle as the temperature falls.

Plastics in modelling

So why use plastics in modelling? Well, it may be that you build plastic models; scale models of aircraft, ships, land vehicles or human figures. But for other types of models, surely wood and metal meet most needs. Well, not quite. Consider the advantages of plastics, as a group of materials,

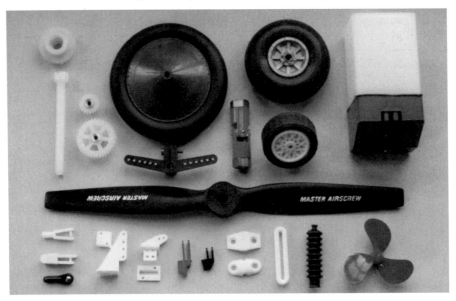

Figure 5 Just a few of the many plastic items used in model aircraft, boats and cars.

listed in Table 1. It is not, however, all good news. Quite often, working with plastics is a smelly business and there is never the beautiful scent of freshly sawn wood. Furthermore, plastics have some less desirable characteristics and these are listed in Table 2.

For the vast majority of uses, the advantages of plastic materials far outweigh their snags and most models these days feature a wide mixture of basic materials in their construction.

The use of plastics can be a great help in the design of new models. The texture of any plastic part can be hard and glossy or soft and non-slip. It can simulate a wide variety of constructional materials including bricks, stone and concrete. The items can be self-coloured and transparent, translucent or opaque. The material can provide built-in hinges or parts that can snap-fit together. Shapes, particularly curves, are easy to form and sheet materials have many variations and uses.

Finally, two notes of caution. First, some additives tend to migrate out of a few plastics in the presence of other chemicals. An example of this is the effect of some paint and self-adhesive decals on polycarbonate crash helmets, which can make the polycarbonate brittle and unable to provide the required level of protection. Of more interest to the modeller is the same effect on polycarbonate model car bodies.

Second, it has been realised for some time that PVC and styrene can react together so that the tyres on plastic car kits may start to melt the wheels after twenty plus years. Certain museums are noting that some of their older plastic materials are starting to exhibit a chemical reaction which causes them to drip a sticky substance, give out a vinegary smell and crack or flake. First to be noticed was the effect on pre-1950s plastic dolls, but a similar effect has now been noticed in early space suits and steering wheels of classic cars among other items. It has also been observed in mid-1970s Barbie dolls and Star Wars figures. Universities are now studying the phenomenon.

Durable
Waterproof
Resistant to most chemicals
Self-finishing
Easily self-coloured all the way through
Light weight combined with high strength
Exceptionally strong in composite form
Good electrical and heat insulators
Easily moulded and shaped
Transparent to radio signals (not carbon fibre composites)
Readily available
Low cost

Table 1 *There are lots of advantages when you use plastics in your models.*

Relatively soft surfaces
Hardest are no better than aluminium
Heat sensitive
Lose strength at 150° C
Melt below 250° C.
A few useable up to 300° C
Creep under load
Build up static electricity causing dust to cling
Often difficult to paint
Many are very inflammable giving off toxic fumes
Liquid plastics are smelly and often toxic
Most are not biodegradable

Table 2 *Plastic materials also have a few short-comings.*

Figure 6 Items made from plastics which occur naturally include old 78 rpm gramophone records, buttons and much ornamental jewellery.

Plastics derived from nature

A few plastics either naturally occur or are obtained from natural sources, rather than the petrochemical industry. Details of them are outlined but their application to modelling is not considered.

Amber

Amber is a natural resin which is still employed as an ingredient in some varnishes. It used to have applications in making cigarette and pipe mouthpieces and is still found in decorative jewellery and ornaments.

Bitumen

Commonly referred to as asphalt, these naturally occurring materials are also a residue of petroleum distillation. They are black and brittle, resist most chemicals, are good electrical insulators and very cheap. Their brittleness is easily reduced by the addition of fibres. They are widely used for road making and as building sealants.

Casein

Casein is a rigid, horn-like substance made from fat-free milk. It is noted for its brilliant colours and ability to simulate natural materials. It is used to make adhesives, buttons, buckles and hair slides.

Natural rubber

Some 2,000 different plants produce rubbery saps but it was the native Brazilian rubber tree which led to the rubber plantations in south-east Asia. Raw latex from these trees is costly and is used to make natural rubber in a variety of grades and forms, including crepe rubber and latex foams.

Rubber has a basic tack, which means that two surfaces brought together will become strongly attached to each other. It is used to make contact adhesives, contraceptives, erasers, rubber gloves and some engineering products such as sewer gaskets and bridge bearings. Most rubber, however, is vulcanised by the addition of sulphur for use as vehicle tyres.

Shellac

Shellac comes from the secretion of a parasitic insect found in India and south-east Asia. It was very widely used to make old-fashioned 78rpm gramophone records, with other applications in the furnishing industry and home-care products as French and floor polishes.

It is still used to make sealing wax and some adhesives.

Part 1 – Types of plastic materials

There will, I promise, be no exam at the end of this chapter on the names of the various plastics. The reason for giving the complete names is that some readers may find this interesting and it indicates where each plastic fits into the wide range.

There are well over a hundred commercially available plastics, with new and improved ones being added to the list each year, as well as blends of several plastics. However, four plastics presently account for 75% of current production. These four are polyethylene (commonly called polythene), polypropylene, PVC and the styrenes including polystyrene and ABS.

This book does not try to cover every single plastic but, as well as looking at the main ones, covers other less common ones which are still very useful to the modeller. This book uses the term polythene to describe polyethylene, styrene for the basic plastic modelling material but polystyrene and expanded polystyrene for the consumer materials.

It is important to recognise that during the development of plastics, many new materials have been given trade names by their producers, rather than relying on generic plastic names to describe them. Some of these are registered trademarks but, for simplicity, the ® symbol is omitted. Brief details of the ones that you are likely to come across are included in this chapter.

As mentioned earlier, plastics are loosely categorised into two groups, based on their physical characteristics. Thermoplastics can be, and repeatedly are, melted down and remoulded. Thermosetting plastics or thermosets, on the other hand, cannot be remelted making them more suitable for applications where heat is encountered.

In examining the commonly found plastics, an indication is given of the useful properties of each one together with a list of its common uses and an illustration of a typical modelling application. This should help to identify which plastics are best for which modelling applications.

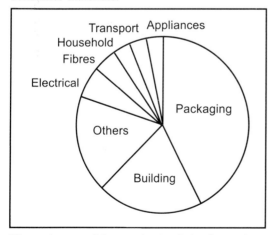

The main use of thermoplastics is in the packaging and building industries.

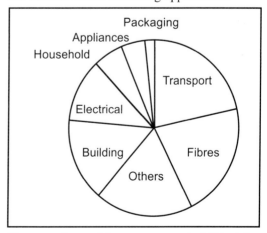

The rate of use of thermosets is only 15% of that of thermoplastics.

Chapter 1 Thermoplastics and thermosetting plastics

Thermoplastics

You can distinguish thermoplastics as they are easy to liquefy or reshape using heat and you can recycle them by melting them down and filling fresh moulds with them. For modellers, the ability to heat form and vacuum form this category of plastic materials makes them a particularly attractive proposition.

ABS (acrylonitrile butadiene styrene)

Typical uses – cameras, vehicle interior fittings, housings for consumer electronics, shavers, telephones.

ABS features a fine combination of impact resistance, rigidity and toughness. It is easy to form and the resulting item can have a superior surface finish to other plastics. It is low cost, though it is not transparent. Its lack of weather resistance means applications tend to be limited to interior environments, but otherwise it has good chemical resistance. It is widely used for components in model aircraft and boat kits and with some justification. Many of the materials in the Plastruct range are made from grey ABS.

Acetal (polyacetal)

Typical uses – gears, sprockets, blower wheels, pump impellers, fan blades, shower heads and plumbing valve components.

This good-looking white material is quite a dense plastic and has excellent mechanical properties combined with good chemical resistance. Its dimensional stability allows it to be used to make close tolerance parts and its moisture absorption is relatively low, as is its coefficient of friction. It can withstand boiling water (up to 115°C) and is

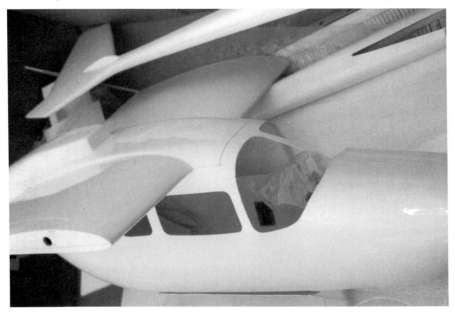

Figure 1.1 A kit for a flying model aircraft made almost entirely from ABS.

a slow burning material. These are similar characteristics to nylon but with very much less water absorption and better abrasion resistance. Acetal is used in engineering applications where these two characteristics are needed and is also found in plumbing fittings. Most acetal is injection moulded, only 5% being extruded in sheet or rod form for subsequent machining.

Delrin

Delrin is a Du Pont proprietary form of acetal which is rather better for machining and has superior mechanical properties, apart from its resistance to hot water and alkaline liquids. You should use black Delrin when the material is exposed to sunlight and the black colour is unimportant.

Duracon

This is another popular proprietary acetal, mainly used for making injection-moulded gears.

Acrylic (polymethyl methacrylate)

Typical uses – baths and wash basins, car light covers, display signs, light fittings, safety glass, spectacles and lenses, motor cycle windscreens. Though this plastic is also found in paints, clothing and adhesives, the most widely known form

Figure 1.2 An acetal blower with aluminium hub.

is perspex, but there are many other variations of the material which are popular for moulding rigid shapes. Clear, translucent and opaque types are easily obtained in literally thousands of different colours. In its clear form, it outperforms most types of glass. It can be extruded to form light pipes which will transmit a high proportion of light along their length regardless of bends. The edges of sheet material appear luminous.

Figure 1.3 A display case, made of wood and perspex, protects this scratch-built Reliant Robin.

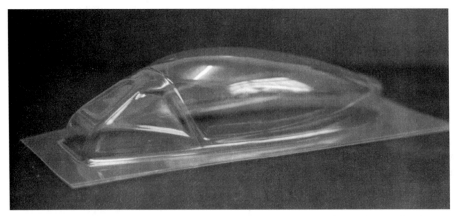

Figure 1.4 A cellulose aircraft cockpit for a model Spitfire. (Photo courtesy Vortex Plastics)

It is a hard, rigid, somewhat brittle substance with an excellent surface finish which weathers and machines well but does absorb a small percentage of water when immersed.

Perspex

Polymethyl acrylate or perspex was first produced in the UK in 1934 and, because of its shatterproof characteristics and its clear optical properties, an early use was for the canopies and gun turrets of Hurricanes, Spitfires and Lancasters.

Cellulose plastics (celluloid)

Typical uses – combs, fibres, films, lacquers, table tennis balls, toothbrushes, tool handles.

Cellulose is an abundant natural material found in many forms of plant life. Prolific sources are the cotton plant and tree wood. One of the earliest plastics to find widespread use, its popularity today is much reduced and rates of production of the material minimal. This is mainly due to its high inflammability and poor chemical properties.

All the cellulose-based plastics are very tough and well able to resist impacts. They also have an excellent appearance and are available as transparent sheets which are easy to vacuum form.

Cellulose acetate (acetate)

Compared with vinyls, cellulose acetate plastic features high water absorption, poor electrical characteristics, limited resistance to heat and to ageing. It is widely used as the basis of the photographic film in your camera. It is also commonly used in dope for shrinking coverings on flying model aircraft. Cinemoid should be familiar to amateur dramatics enthusiasts and is a range of self-extinguishing acetate sheet used for colouring incandescent and fluorescent lighting.

This plastic is available in a transparent form as acetate sheet, is low cost and used for many vacuum-formed commercial canopies. It is weather resistant, easy to mould and resulting shapes have good optical properties.

Cellulose acetate butyrate (butyrate)

CAB (cellulose acetate butyrate), often called just butyrate, is a much improved variant of cellulose with lower water absorption and better flow properties than cellulose acetate. It is pliable, machinable and very durable. The Plastruct range includes a selection of white butyrate tubing and fittings. It is ideal for representing glass or perspex in any model and may be used for aircraft canopies, car and boat windscreens and glazing for buildings.

Cellulose nitrate

Cellulose nitrate is renowned for its flammability and would be a hazard in many modelling applications. It has a distinctive smell of camphor (used as a plasticiser) and is fairly uncommon these days. It is probably only found in modelling because it is still used to make table tennis balls.

Polyamides

Nylon

Typical uses – clothes, curtain rails, gears, nuts and bolts, zips.

Nylon is by far the most common aliphatic polyamide material and is available in several distinctive forms. In its fibre form the thread is often used for rigging boats and as kite string. As a fabric, it is used for making sails and provides a tough covering for kites and larger flying model aircraft. It can also be used for dressing larger scale figures.

In its solid form it is an important engineering material and is used in many load-bearing applications, but tends to absorb moisture. It has a low coefficient of friction and machines well. It is tough, rigid, heat resistant and also relatively unaffected by oils, greases and abrasion; better than most non-ferrous metals!

It is used to make items such as bearings, bushes, cams, gears, rollers, and valve seats as well as model-size propellers both for aircraft and boats. It is also made into monofilament fishing line, cords and ropes, electrical mouldings and cable coverings.

Its more widespread use has been limited by the fact that it is three times the price of polythene and polystyrene.

Nylon 66

This nylon is white and has a high melting point (260°C), as well as excellent mechanical properties, good electrical characteristics and resistance to chemicals.

Glass-filled nylon 66

Increased strength and stiffness is provided by this 30% glass 70% nylon mix. Dark grey in colour, it can withstand temperatures of 110°C continuously and 200°C for short periods.

Cast nylon 6

A natural-coloured material, it is ideal for machining as it is free of internal stresses. It has a high abrasion resistance and is unaffected by most chemicals including salt water.

MoS^2 filled cast nylon 6

This variant of cast nylon is black as it has molybdenum disulphide incorporated, resulting in a low-friction material which is self-lubricating. It is tough, abrasion resistant and has a relatively high melting point (230°C).

Nylatron GS

Nylatron GS is a nylon 66 based material with molybdenum disulphide added. It has similar

Figure 1.5 Nylon gear wheels and pulleys on sale at an exhibition.

properties to MoS^2 filled cast nylon 6 but is significantly more expensive.

Nyloil

This is a creamy yellow oil-filled nylon with a much lower coefficient of friction than any other form of nylon. It is free-cutting, allowing machining to tight tolerances and smooth finishes. It has a high resistance to water absorption.

Kevlar

Typical uses – body armour, helmets, pressure vessels, rocket motors and tyres.

Kevlar is from the same chemical family as nylon and is an aromatic polyamide fibre, first produced

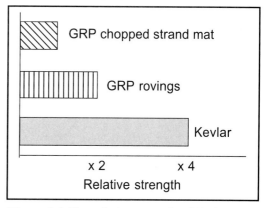

Figure 1.6 The relative strength of Kevlar compared to other composite materials.

by Du Pont. It is known for its strength, light weight and resistance to stretching. It is available in the form of cloth or as a cord.

Torlon

Torlon has exceptional physical and chemical characteristics and will operate for long periods at up to 230°C, but is badly attacked by steam at 160°C. It is very strong in compression and has a high impact resistance. It has a low coefficient of expansion and good chemical resistance.

Bearing grade

This greeny black material has graphite and fluorocarbon added to provide low friction, good wear resistance and high compressive strength. Able to operate for long periods at 230°C, it is ideal for applications such as bearings, piston rings, thrust washers and wear pads.

Electrical grade

Coloured dark brown, this material is an excellent electrical insulator and is widely used in connectors, relays and switches.

Tufnol

Tufnol has excellent mechanical and electrical properties and low water absorption. It is brown in colour and widely available in a number of different forms with varying properties.

Carp brand

This brand of tufnol is a brown laminate based on a fine weave, quality fabric. It is used for small-toothed gears and other precision components.

Kite brand

This is a readily machinable form of tufnol available in rod and sheet form. It is widely used for electrical items due to its excellent high voltage insulation properties. It can also be drilled and tapped.

Whale brand

A medium weave, quality fabric-laminated plastic available in sheet and rod forms

10G/40

An epoxy glass laminate supplied in rod form, it has extremely high electrical and mechanical performance. It has good insulation characteristics regardless of wide variations in humidity and is rigid and dimensionally stable.

Polycarbonate

Typical uses – CDs, covers for batteries and time switches, food processor bowls, glazing, microwave cookware, safety goggles and helmets.

This is the strongest of the mouldable plastics. It is transparent with a low rate of water absorption and high stain resistance. It is also the hardest to form and the most expensive by a factor of two. It will withstand the highest temperatures (140°C) and is virtually self-extinguishing. It has limited resistance to chemicals and ultra-violet light. Its toughness and flexibility lend it to the manufacture of a wide range of commercial and domestic items.

Figure 1.7 An unpainted polycarbonate car body shows off the interior detail.

Corotherm

This transparent polycarbonate material has been developed as an alternative to glass for making insulated roofing for conservatories. It comes in a range of thickness from 6mm to 16mm and is shatter- and environment-proof. It is easily cut with a Stanley knife. It should be cleaned with soapy water as it is scratched by abrasive cleaners.

Corex

A semi-rigid hollow plastic, it needs tensioning to provide a flat surface. It is light with an excellent surface finish but must have its edges taped when used as a boat decking material to avoid water ingress to its hollow interior.

Lexan

A tough polycarbonate produced by General Electric of the US, it is popular for R/C helicopter canopies and car bodies. It is transparent and can be painted with special polycarbonate paints, available from model shops. It is often painted on the inside to allow the material itself to provide a glossy, hard-wearing finish.

Polyester

Typical uses – audio and video tapes, coffee makers, fizzy drinks bottles, textiles, toasters, paints and varnishes.

The information here refers to polyester in its thermoplastic form. Polyester in its thermosetting form is covered in the next section of this chapter. Polyester is the material used to make blow-moulded bottles for carbonated drinks. It is also used as a basis for most domestic paints and varnishes. Copolyesters are variations of polyester made by reaction with other materials. A common form is clear copolyester sheet which can withstand temperatures up to 250°C and is pliable and stress resistant.

In its fibre form, polyester thread is woven into a useful material called terylene (Dacron in the US). Fabrics woven from these threads are widely used but lack stretch resistance on the bias (diagonally to the weave).

Mylar and melinex

Better stretch resistance results from bonding a thin film of polyester to the woven cloth. The laminate may be a film of polyester between layers of terylene, layers of film with a layer of terylene between or just a layer of each. It is the basis of some modellers' iron-on covering materials.

Polyethylene (polythene)

Typical uses – bin liners, carrier bags, disposable cups, food storage containers, gas and water pipes, kitchenware, toys and TV cabinets.

Polyethylene (normally contracted in the UK to polythene) is the most widely produced plastic and as a result is low in price. It is a wax-like material which has good resistance to chemicals, is a good insulator and does not absorb water. It is tough and flexible, but not very strong in tension. It does, however, scratch easily and softens at temperatures between 80 and 130° C. It is inflammable and burns producing plenty of smoke. It is slightly less dense than water and thus all forms of this plastic float. It is available in rod, sheet and block forms. In some thin film grades, it is transparent.

The fact that there are two main variants of polythene – high density and low density – is not a major concern. There are many additives which will alter the characteristics of the basic material. These include fillers and colour pigments, flame retarders and anti-static agents.

From a modeller's point of view, polythene sheeting is ideal for protecting plans in the workshop, and work surfaces and walls when spray

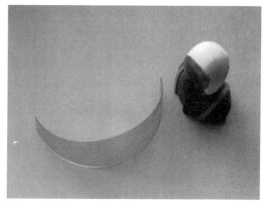

Figure 1.8 Part of a polyester drinks bottle makes an excellent windscreen or pilot's visor.

painting. Many food containers and bottles are useful for storing modelling materials and some items find their way into the models themselves – yoghurt pots cut to represent jet pipes on flying aircraft models and polythene water pipes for model submarines.

Polypropylene
Typical uses – biscuit wrappers, car parts, kettles, luggage, margarine tubs, rope, string and netting, toilet cisterns, washing-up bowls.

Polypropylene has many similar characteristics to polythene but is harder and has a glossier finish. It is also less dense and has a higher melting point by some 50° C (it will withstand boiling water for a limited period).

Its impact strength leaves something to be desired and it becomes brittle around freezing temperatures. It is widely used for making injection-moulded items. A particularly useful characteristic is its resistance to fatigue when flexed (and stress cracking) making it a good hinging material. It is commonly used both for hinges and hinged containers. In sheet form, it is the plastic from which Solarfilm, the heat-shrink covering material is manufactured.

As with polythene, additives are often used to modify the properties of polypropylene. These include fillers, rubbers and colourings and are used to increase impact strength, thermal stability, fatigue strength, reduce stiffness and brighten colour. Polypropylene is available in

perforated sheet form which resists most industrial chemicals.

Polystyrene (styrene)
Typical uses – household goods, plastic models, toys.

Polystyrene is available in two main forms; solid and expanded. It is cheap, easy to form and is widely used for unstressed injection mouldings. It is a hard, rigid, transparent material which gives off a metallic ring when struck. It is low cost, easy to mould and is readily coloured. It is widely used to make toys, domestic items and packaging.

It produces smoke when burned and is attacked or dissolved by many liquids. It tends to be brittle and cannot withstand boiling water. It is marginally denser than water and is not very resistant to oils.

Both high impact and toughened versions of polystyrene are produced, particularly for household goods and a wide range of toys. This is the material used for making small plastic model kits by companies like Airfix. It is usually sold in white sheets and is cheap to buy, strong, gives excellent mould detail and is readily available in sheets of varying thickness.

Evergreen, Plastruct and Plasticard
These three are well-known commercial names in the modelling field which include a wide range of white styrene sheet and shaped building materials.

Figure 1.9 A polythene tank is ideal for holding the fuel for a model car, boat or aircraft.

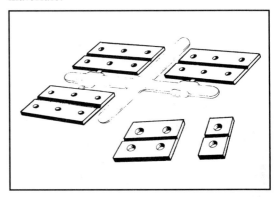

Figure 1.10 Simple and inexpensive one-part polypropylene hinges come in a variety of lengths. (Picture courtesy Chart)

Expanded polystyrene

Typical uses – building insulation, egg and hamburger boxes, protective packaging.

Expanded polystyrene is inert, odourless and non-toxic. It has an exceptionally low thermal conductivity and low density but is rather brittle. It is widely used for packaging new equipment and in modelling for applications as varied as aircraft wings and building up scenic layouts.

A very lightweight material in this form, expanded polystyrene is best cut to shape with a hot wire, though you can use a sharp serrated knife or razor saw. It is widely employed for flying model parts and is available in a white form and as a denser blue type, which is twice as heavy. Foam densities vary, but a typical figure for white foam is 20gm/1000cc.

PTFE (polytetrafluoroethylene)

Typical uses – bearings, lubricant additive, non-stick cookware surface coating.

PTFE, also called teflon or fluon, is a dense and expensive plastic. It has an exceptionally low co-efficient of friction (values range from 0.02 - 0.1), making it ideal for lightly-stressed bearings, as a powdered additive to lubricants and as a surface coating. It resists almost all chemicals; no other plastic is so resistant. It can withstand relatively high temperatures (250°C) as well as exceptionally low ones. It is a also superb insulator.

It is most commonly found as a coating for non-stick saucepans. It is readily machined,

though you must take care as it starts to decompose at 270°C, producing poisonous fumes. You should never smoke when machining it as you could draw in dust from the machining process.

PTFE tape is the normal material used by plumbers to seal waterproof joints where soldered or compression joints cannot be employed. Wrapped round the male portion before insertion into the female part, it acts as a first-class jointing material. It is also employed in numerous seals, gaskets, packings, valves and pump parts.

Viton

The viton O-rings, used in steam locomotive glands, are a form of PTFE and, as a result, can liberate very dangerous fumes if seriously overheated.

PVA (polyvinyl acetate)

Typical uses – adhesives, emulsion paints, release agent for composite materials, textiles, water-soluble packaging.

PVA is soluble in water and slightly denser. It has a high tensile strength and is very tough. It is resistant to hydrocarbons such as petrol and alcohols, providing the latter do not contain water. While its main uses are in liquid form in

Figure 1.11 The parts of this Tornado, made from a plastic kit, are formed from polystyrene.

Figure 1.12 The vertical rod of this hot air engine moves in a PTFE bearing.

Figure 1.13 Containers of PVA woodworkers' glue and GRP release agent.

Figure 1.14 An expanded polystyrene piston in a hot air engine.

glues and paints, when made into fibres, it is widely employed in the furnishing industry.

PVC or vinyl (polyvinyl chloride)

Typical uses – bottles and containers, cable insulation, clingfilm, clear sheeting, drain pipes and gutters, floor coverings, leather cloth and window frames.

PVC is one of the most widely produced plastics. It is harder than polythene and has better resistance to burning. It is commonly found in two forms, UPVC (unplasticised PVC) and PPVC (plasticised). However, CPVC (chlorinated PVC) is becoming increasingly popular, mainly due to its resistance to combustion distortion at higher temperatures.

The amount of plasticiser added to the raw material varies from a little in UPVC (unplasticised) to a high proportion in flexible versions which also soften at fairly low temperatures. PVC is resistant to corrosion and abrasive scratching. It is used to make water piping, inflatable goods like beach mattresses and a range of containers and electrical fittings as well as sheet material. It is widely used in the building industry for drain pipes and guttering, not to mention replacement windows.

Clear corrugated sheet has recently emerged as a fine material for moulding transparent components. It is cheap, widely available, and the ease with which you can shape it by just heating it and pulling it over a form make it a good choice.

Plasticised PVC is the form used as the covering for electric flex, hose pipes, leather cloth and clingfilm. Finally, mention must be made of hot-melt vinyl which is specially formulated for making rubber moulds.

Fablon

A PVC-based, self-adhesive plastic film material, Fablon is available in a wide range of colours and patterns which include baize and simulated wood.

Thermosetting plastics

Basically, thermosetting plastics are formed by chemical reactions which take place during the moulding or forming process. Thus, while you can cut scrap materials to shape, you cannot reform them. Their attractiveness from a modelling point of view lies in the ability to start the chemical reaction exactly when and where you need it. Thermosetting plastics are the basis of all composite materials.

Acrylic

Typical uses – adhesives, laminating resins.
Of all the acrylic-based adhesives, the cyanoacrylates or superglues are by far the most widely used. These glues work very rapidly when exposed to moisture but have no fundamental gap-filling capabilities. Their shelf life is measured in months, providing they are stored in dry air. Chapter 4 indicates the various ways in which you can enhance the cure time and gap-filling capabilities of these glues.

The anaerobic properties of thermosetting acrylics are used in engineering where it is the absence of air between, for example, two mild steel surfaces, together with the presence of iron, which activates the glue. Acrylic resins are starting to compete with polyester for laminating, their advantage being a lower rate of shrinkage.

Epoxy

Typical uses – adhesives, floor laminates, GRP, carbon fibre and Kevlar composites, encapsulation of electronic components, surface coatings.
Epoxy resins are cold setting and will survive quite high temperatures. There are many different hardening systems which vary pot life, cure time and the attributes of the cured material. Their important characteristics include good adhesion to metals, very high electrical resistance, low shrinkage (much lower than polyester resins),

Figure 1.15 *A PVC-covered seat on a model traction engine's trailer.*

Figure 1.16 *Acrylic glues give good adhesion on many plastics. (Photo courtesy Deluxe Materials)*

toughness and machinability. In the modelling world the most common application is as an adhesive. Araldite is probably the best known of these two-part adhesives and is available with a range of setting speeds.

Epoxies are used for surface coating of model aircraft and boats, and also as potting materials for electronics and for making small moulds. Two-part epoxy putties like Ferro-plast and Milliput have the consistency of plasticine when mixed and they set hard enough to be machined, drilled and tapped.

Phenolic

Typical uses – adhesives, electric iron parts, laminates, lamp housings, plugs and switches, saucepan handles, surface coatings.

The phenolics are a family of hard, heat-resisting plastics which are also resistant to chemical attack. They are stable up to 200°C with some claiming to withstand short-term exposure to

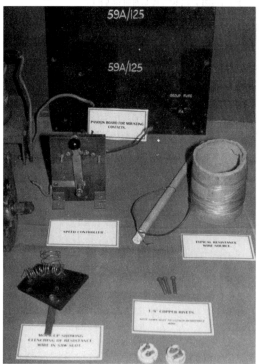

***Figure 1.17** Paxolin is a phenolic laminate widely used in components of electric drive systems.*

300°C. Their electrical insulation properties are adequate provided the humidity is low.

Bakelite

Phenol formaldehyde (PF) is commonly known as Bakelite and is one of the oldest plastics. Its dark colour is typical of this class of plastics. It is a cheap, rigid material which still has uses in the electrical/electronics world.

Phenolic laminates

Typical uses – ashtrays, decorative laminates, tableware.

These laminates are strong, rigid, machinable and are available in sheet, tube and moulded form. Their dark colour makes them unsuitable as decorative laminates unless given a top layer of melamine. However under the name paxolin, they are still used in the electrical and electronic industries in the manufacture of insulators and many printed circuit boards.

Formica

A popular decorative phenolic laminate coated with melamine, the most popular modelling use of formica is as a work surface for power tools in the workshop. It is relatively heat-proof and very easy to clean. You should remember, if using it in a model or as a model base, that it is quite a heavyweight material.

Formaldehydes (aminos)

Both melamine formaldehyde (MF) and urea formaldehyde (UF) are very hard and tough materials. They have good abrasion resistance and are self-extinguishing if exposed to a naked flame

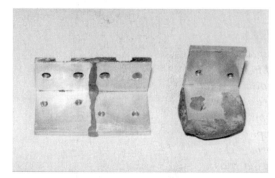

***Figure 1.18** Ferro-plast epoxy putty will fix to most materials and is easily drilled and tapped.*

which is subsequently removed. Glass- and metal-filled variants are quite dense.

MF (melamine formaldehyde)

Typical uses – surface coating for laminates and boards, tableware.

This plastic is used as a popular surface layer for decorative laminates such as melamine-coated chip-board. This is because it is very hard, scratch and stain resistant. Due to its expense, melamine is only used as a coating on laminates made from the phenols, such as formica.

UF (urea formaldehyde)

Typical uses – bathroom equipment, electrical plugs, food trays, switches and sockets.

The popularity of UF, when it was first introduced, was due to its unusually wide colour range. It is a better insulator than the phenolics as it does not promote surface electrical tracking when damp. As a result, although less heat resistant, it is used to make most domestic plugs, sockets and switches. It does not impart taste or odour to food or drink. It is, however, only heat resistant up to 70°C. UF also makes an excellent wood adhesive and is widely used in the manufacture of chip-

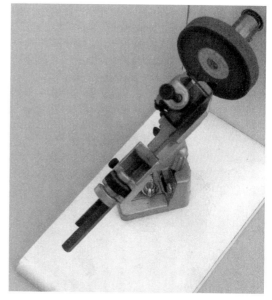

Figure 1.19 This drill-sharpening rig is mounted on an offcut of formica, a phenolic laminate with a formaldehyde surface coating.

board. It is often used near to naked flames and to cover a range of composite wood materials.

Figure 1.20 This large model diesel locomotive shows a typical application of formaldehyde-based plastic in its electrical switches.

Because, in its raw state, UF is very white, it is easily brightly coloured.

In a foam form, it is used to fill the gap in cavity walls. These foams are also used in flower decoration, as artificial snow and on airport runways for emergency landings.

Polyester

Typical uses – GRP resin, engineering materials.
Probably the most common use of thermosetting polyester is as the resin for making composite materials such as glass reinforced plastic. It is significantly cheaper than epoxy resin, but does emit a strong smell which many people find objectionable. Polyester resins are slightly coloured and are mixed with a catalyst, usually an organic peroxide paste. They set fairly quickly but the ultimate strength of the composite will take days to develop. Densities of the finished GRP items lie in the range 1.4 - 2 g/cc³, depending on the form of glass used and the method of construction; hand laid-up mat being at the light end of the range. Polyester is also found in a variety of forms and Victrex is a typical example of a tough polyester-based engineering material.

Isopon
Isopon is the trade name of an easily sanded polyester-based filler which is widely used to repair

dents and scratches in car bodies. It also useful for undertaking similar repairs in GRP models.

Victrex
Victrex, a commercial form of PEEK (polyether ether ketone), is closely related to the acetal family. It is a high-performance engineering plastic which is strong and rigid. It has exceptional high temperature characteristics being able to be used at 250°C. It can withstand steam and high pressure water applications and is highly resistant to most liquids.

Polyurethane

Typical uses – car bumpers, diaphragms, foam for soft furnishings, forklift truck tyres, varnishes, rubber for oil seals, shoe soles and heels.
By varying the proportions of the two constituent parts forming these plastics, the characteristics can be varied to provide adhesives, foams, moulded sheets, rubbers and surface coatings.

Polyurethanes are commonly made into foamed materials. Polyurethane foam, though twice the weight of expanded polystyrene, has even better insulation properties and is flexible. It has applications in modelling both as rigid and flexible foam as well as providing an excellent buoyancy material. Polyurethane resin is an

Figure 1.21 A pair of GRP cowls will house the engines of this flying scale model.

Figure 1.22 Polyurethane round and toothed belts are popular for driving machinery.

alternative to polyester resin as a casting material. Polyurethane rubbers have exceptional tensile strength, tear and abrasion resistance, but are quite hard and not very resilient, lying somewhere between flexible thermoplastics and conventional rubbers.

Tufset

Tufset is a rigid pale-blue polyurethane plastic with good dimensional stability and high abrasion resistance. It is also relatively fatigue free and resists stress cracking. It is easily machined to close tolerances with a quality finish. It resists most chemicals and other environmental conditions, direct sunlight only slowly causing yellowing. It is used as an insulator by the electrical industry and is also good for making bearings, bushes, cams, gears, guides, pads and wear strips.

Silicone

There is a complete family of silicone products which includes both rubbers and liquids. The liquids are marginally less dense than water while the rubbers are quite dense.

Silicone rubber

Typical uses – flexible figures and tubing, gaskets, mould making, seals and sealants, potting and encapsulation.

Room-temperature vulcanising silicone rubbers are elastic, heat-resistant and exhibit low shrinkage. They are incompatible with most other materials, making them ideal for flexible moulds. They also have good electrical properties. They are, however, quite expensive and have a relatively short shelf life – measured in months. Most silicone rubbers are two-part materials, but silicone bath sealant is a one-part rubber, which emits a smell of vinegar as it cures. The four silicone rubbers detailed below, all two-part, are made by General Electric of the USA and are available from Alec Tiranti.

RTV-11

This is a white, free-flowing, general-purpose rubber which is ideal for making firm yet flexible moulds where there is no excessive undercut. It is cured by the addition of DBT and will withstand continuous exposure to 200°C and occasional exposure to 260°C.

RTV-31

A red rubber, this is the firmest of the four when cured and can survive the highest temperatures; continuously 260°C, occasionally 315°C. It is thus ideal as a mould material for low-melt temperature metals. It is normally cured by the addition of DBT.

RTV-420

This white pourable condensation-cure rubber has a high strength and tear resistance yet is soft, flexible and ideal for deep undercuts. It is particularly well suited to making skin moulds when thickened with Tixo TA1 thixotropic agent.

RTV-428

This is another white pourable condensation-cure rubber, also with high strength and tear resistance, which is rather firmer than RTV-420. Again, it can be thickened with the thixotropic agent.

Catalysts for silicone rubber

There are three catalysts which are mixed with the silicone rubber to enable it to cure. Which of these

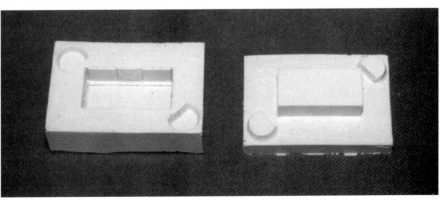

Figure 1.23 A silicone rubber mould for the body of an N gauge railway wagon.

Figure 1.24 Synthetic rubber tyres fitted to radio controlled cars.

you choose depends on the grade of rubber you select and your desired cure time. The three are:

Dibutyl tin dilaurate (DBT)
Transparent Beta 7
Blue Beta 11 D1

Tixo TA1 thixotropic additive

This is a clear liquid which you can add to the RTV-400 range of rubbers to make them thixotropic (non-drip) when they are being painted onto forms.

Cab-O-Sil

This is a filler for silicone rubber, which makes it thicker, stronger and thixotropic.

Maestro acrylic/PVA polymers

Maestro polymer colouring materials are available in a wide range of tints as an additive to silicone rubbers and you can even use them to paint cured rubber.

DP 100

A silicone rubber release agent for treatment of mould boxes, it is normally supplied as an aerosol spray.

Silicone fluid

Typical uses – additives to paints and polishes, barrier creams, lubricants and greases, release agents, water-repellent coatings.

These fluids are anti-stick, water-repellent and have low surface tension making their use widespread.

SF-96-50 silicone fluid

This fluid may be used to thin silicone rubber and is also a good liquid for cleaning bushes covered in catalysed silicone rubber.

Synthetic rubber (diene and olefin rubbers)

Typical uses – O-rings, seals and vehicle tyres.
Along with natural rubber, made from plant latex, SBR is the most widely used synthetic rubber. A wide range of other specialist rubbers, a term meaning not suitable for tyres, exists and includes materials such as CR (chloroprene rubber) and BR (butadiene rubber).

SBR (styrene-butadiene rubber)

SBR is a low-cost and hard-wearing synthetic rubber which can easily be produced to a uniform consistency. It also has better low temperature properties than natural rubber but does not exhibit natural tack and, with age, does eventually become hard and brittle. Like natural rubber, it can also be vulcanised and is widely used, among other things, for making tyres for the automobile industry.

NBR (nitrile rubber)

NBR has similar properties to SBR and is often used to make O-rings.

Klingersil

This material is a composite synthetic jointing material, available in three grades, all of which contain NBR. It is expensive but is ideal for use with air, steam, oils and fuels. Depending on the grade, it will withstand steam up to 290°C, a maximum temperature of 450°C and pressures up to 130 bar.

The grades comprise:

- A compressed fibre jointing material in sheet form with anti-stick surfaces, incorporating glass fibre with a nitrile rubber binder. One side of the sheet is green; the other white.
- A green compressed synthetic fibre gasket material of aramid fibres with a nitrile rubber binder, designed for use in internal combustion engines and compressors.
- A black, compressed synthetic-fibre jointing material which is a direct alternative to asbestos. It is made from carbon fibre in a nitrile-rubber binder. It is ideal for hot, high-pressure steam applications.

CR (chloroprene rubber)

CR is the leading synthetic rubber not used for making tyres. It has better resistance to oils and heat than SBR or NBR. It is still used for adhesives, automobile applications and wire covering.

Neoprene

Du Pont's neoprene is a chloroprene rubber which is airtight, and quite resistant to the effects of heat and burning. It is also relatively impervious to the effects of petrol and oil. In both sheet and tube form, it is particularly popular with model engineers working with internal combustion engines.

'I KNOW IT TAKES UP A LOT OF ROOM....
...BUT YOU NEVER KNOW WHEN IT'LL COME IN USEFUL!'

Chapter 2 Basic forms of plastics

Identification of plastics

Identifying which plastic has been used to make any commercial item is sometimes difficult, particularly if your aim is to recover and re-use the material. The reasons for needing to identify the actual plastic include its suitability for its new role and the best adhesives for fixing it in place.

Some re-use, like the conversion of a plastic bottle into a pressurised air storage container is quite straightforward. For other requirements, the initial use of the object may well indicate the type of plastic used in its manufacture or may, by its application, indicate some of the likely characteristics such as toughness, heat or chemical resistance. You will need to think about whether such characteristics are important in the new role you envisage for the material. If you are planning to glue it, a simple adhesive test may suffice.

Visual and mechanical testing

Often the feel or colour of the plastic is a give-away but sometimes you may want to do a more rigorous series of tests such as those listed below.

1. Does a sample float or sink in water?
2. Is it rigid or flexible?
3. Is it transparent or opaque and is it coloured?
4. What is the surface finish like, does it feel slippery or waxy and does it resist abrasion?
5. Does it soften and bend when heated?
6. It you bend it backwards and forwards, how easily does it fracture?
7. Is it tough and impact resistant or brittle?

Unfortunately, the last few of these tests destroy a significant sized sample, so it is a good idea to start the tests in numerical order. Table 2.1 shows the characteristics of the main plastics.

	ABS	Acetal	Acrylic	Cellulose	Nylon	Polycarbonate
Floats/sinks in water	=	S	S	S	=	S
Rigid/flexible	F	R	F/R	F	F/R	F
Transparent			✓	✓		✓
Good surface finish	✓	Slippery	✓		Slippery	
Abrasion resistant		✓			✓	✓
Heat formable	✓		✓	✓		✓
Resists stress fracture		✓			✓	✓
Tough	✓	✓	✓	✓	✓	✓
Impact resistant or brittle	I	I		I	I	I

Table 2.1 The properties of plastics likely to help with their identification.

	PVC	Polystyrene	Polyester	Polythene	Polypropylene
Floats/sinks in water	S	=	S	F	F
Rigid/flexible	F	R	F	F	F
Transparent	✓	✓	✓	✓	
Good surface finish	✓		✓	Waxy	✓
Abrasion resistant	✓				
Heat formable	✓	✓			
Resists stress fracture	✓			✓	✓
Tough	✓	✓	✓	✓	✓
Impact resistant or brittle	I	B			B@ <0°C

Table 2.1 continued

	PTFE	Phenolic	Formaldehyde	Polyurethane	SBR
Floats/sinks in water	S	S	S	F	S
Rigid/flexible	R	R	R	F	F
Transparent					
Good surface finish	Slippery	✓	✓		
Abrasion resistant		✓	✓	✓	✓
Heat formable					
Resists stress fracture			✓	✓	
Tough		✓	✓	✓	
Impact resistant or brittle					B with age

Table 2.1 continued

If still in doubt, examine the descriptions of the various materials given in Chapter 1.

Flame testing

Because many plastics have a similar appearance and colouring, holding a small sample in a naked flame may assist you in identifying the material. Does it, for example, char or burn easily? Does it produce molten drips? What type of smoke and smell, if any, result from the burning?

The information given in Table 2.2 may help in identification, particularly if you keep labelled samples of known plastics for comparison. A meagre sample will last some time if you only use small amounts in your tests. A green flame means the plastic contains chlorine or fluorine unless it results from colouring or printing on the plastic, particularly blue colours.

For these tests, use small samples, hold them in tongs or tweezers, wear protective gloves and work in a well-ventilated area clear of any other inflammable materials.

Synthetic rubbers
The distinctive smell of burning natural rubber should enable you to distinguish it from the various types of synthetic rubber. You can use small

samples of synthetic rubber seals or O-rings of known types to compare the various different sorts of synthetic rubber.

Solvent tests
A test for polythene or PTFE is that acrylic glues will not join them. You can identify expanded polystyrene visually or by the fact that it rapidly dissolves in petroleum-based solvents. Chloroform is a solvent which only welds acrylic materials. Take care! It is also an anaesthetic and difficult to obtain.

	Acrylic	Cellulose acetate	Nylon	Polycarbonate
Softens/melts in flame	✓			
Chars		✓	✓ & bubbles	✓
Requires strong heating		✓		✓
Burns in flame	Vigorously	✓	✓	✓
Flame	Clear, light yellow			
Produces smoke		✓		✓
Molten drops			✓	
Smell of vapour	Fruity (perspex)	Vinegary	Burning wool	Very little

	Polystyrene	Polythene	Polyurethane	PTFE	PVC
Softens/melts in flame	✓	✓	✓	✓	
Chars			✓		✓
Requires strong heating					
Burns in flame	✓	✓	Only in flame	No	✓
Flame	Very smoky		Discoloured	Green edges	Green edges
Produces smoke	✓	No			✓ Lots
Molten drops		✓			
Smell of vapour	Sweet, sickly	Waxy	Acrid	Poisonous	Choking

Table 2.2 Some of the characteristics of plastics, when placed in a flame.

Material selection

If you are choosing a plastic for a particular modelling application, whether you are planning to purchase the material or recycle it, there are a number of parameters which may help you to arrive at your final choice. However, it is important to remember that some of the properties of plastics will vary depending on their form. Two examples make this point. Expanded polystyrene is a far lighter material than normal polystyrene. Equally, the properties of polyester depend on whether it is in its thermoplastic or thermosetting form.

Table 2.3 indicates some of the more important properties from a modelling point of view and you should use it to guide your choice. Remember to think about how tough an environment the plastic will face, whether the material be exposed to sudden impacts, such as a power boat hull hitting the bank or whether there will be a high vibration level, such as that generated by an internal combustion engine. Will the plastic be

	ABS	Acetal	Acrylic	Cellulose	Nylon	Polycarbonate
Tough	✓	✓	✓	✓	✓	✓
Impact resistant	✓	✓		✓	✓	✓
Brittleness						
Resistant to stress fracture		✓			✓	✓
Rigid/flexible	F	R	F/R	F	F/R	F
Good surface finish	✓		✓			
Abrasion resistant		✓			✓	✓
Low coefficient of friction		✓			✓	
Heat/vacuum formable	✓		✓	✓		
Heat resistant		✓			✓	✓
Inflammable				✓		
Water absorbing			✓	✓	✓	
Transparent			✓	✓		✓
Fuel / oil resistant		✓			✓	
Good electrical properties					✓	
Machinable		✓	✓		✓	
Density relative to water	=	H	M	M	=	M
Cost	L	H	M	L	H	H

Table 2.3 The key properties of plastics normally of interest to modellers.

	PVC	Polystyrene	Polyester	Polythene	Polypropylene
Tough	✓	✓	✓	✓	✓
Impact resistant	✓				
Brittleness		✓			✓ @ <0°C
Resistant to stress fracture	✓			✓	✓
Rigid/flexible	F	R	F	F	F
Good surface finish	✓		✓	Waxy	✓
Abrasion resistant	✓				
Low coefficient of friction					
Heat/vacuum formable	✓	✓			
Heat resistant					✓
Inflammable		✓		✓	
Water absorbing					
Transparent	✓	✓	✓	✓	
Fuel / oil resistant	✓		✓	✓	✓
Good electrical properties	✓		✓	✓	
Machinable					
Density relative to water	H	=	H	L	L
Cost	L	L	L	L	H

Table 2.3 continued

exposed to fuel, oil or even water contamination and how important is heat resistance? You may wish to form the material using heat alone or vacuum form it. You may want to machine a part from the plastic and its frictional properties will affect its suitability as a bearing surface. If you are working with electrics or electronics, the appropriate insulation properties become important. You can also use the table to try to help you identify a plastic which you are planning to recycle.

If you are planning to use any solvent or adhesive, remember to try it on a test sample before proceeding further. Again refer to Chapter 1 for more detailed information on possible plastics to meet your requirement.

Available shapes and sizes
Sheet
Most plastics are available in sheet form, with sizes as small as 300mm square for styrene purchased from model shops to 1200mm by 2400mm

	PTFE	Phenolic	Formaldehyde	Polyurethane	SBR
Tough		✓	✓	✓	
Impact resistant					
Brittleness					with age
Resistant to stress fracture			✓	✓	
Rigid/flexible	R	R	R	F	F
Good surface finish	✓	✓	✓		
Abrasion resistant		✓	✓	✓	✓
Low coefficient of friction	✓				
Heat/vacuum formable					
Heat resistant	✓	✓	✓		
Inflammable					
Water absorbing					
Transparent					
Fuel / oil resistant	✓	✓	✓	✓	✓
Good electrical properties	✓	✓	✓		
Machinable	✓	✓			
Density relative to water	VH	M/H	H	L	H
Cost	H	L	H	M	L

Table 2.3 continued

for sheets of plastics found in DIY stores. Thickness also varies and will depend on the applications envisaged by the manufacturer; not always what you want as a modeller.

Expanded polystyrene is usually sold in sheets 2400mm x 1200mm, and 50mm or 60mm thick is ideal. These are easily cut by scoring with a Stanley knife for ease of transportation. Smaller sheets are also widely available. If you are building a flying model, avoid the heavier grades of foam as well as recycled material.

There is a huge range of flat styrene sheets in a choice of black, white or a number of colours. There are also embossed sheets simulating brick, a range of stones, pebbles and paving slabs, tiles, planks, and asbestos as well as a variety of roof tiles and corrugated finishes. Scales are around 1:144, 1:72 and 1:44 and are intended to suit railway modelling at 2mm, 4mm and 7mm scales.

ABS sheeting comes as grey or white sheeting and is one of the best materials for heat or vacuum forming.

Foam board

Foam board comprises two sheets of white card with a layer of expanded polystyrene between them. A popular trade name is Polyboard, which you can buy from artist supply shops in quite large sheets, typically 1000mm x 1500mm and 3mm or 5mm thick. It is easily cut to shape and is ideal for constructing model buildings. Other applications include the fuselage and ribs of flying model aircraft.

Paxolin and GRP sheet

Paxolin is normally supplied in small sheets measuring 150mm by 100mm and 1.5, 2.4 or 3mm thick A common form has a copper coating on one or both sides for use when making printed circuit boards (PCBs). GRP sheet, copper coated on one or both sides, is also popular for making PCBs and is much stronger than paxolin.

Acrylic products

Clear acrylic sheet (perspex) is usually supplied with a protective paper covering to avoid scratches and varying in thickness from 0.25mm to 6mm. It is also available as clear rod and even clear balls. Acrylic products are also manufactured in a range of tints or colours.

Transparent coloured sheeting

Thin transparent sheeting is ideal for simulating glazing in buildings and other models. Acetate, acrylic, butyrate, polyester and styrene are all suitable for this task. Transparent coloured sheet is an easy way of giving a coloured light effect to a model. The best material for this purpose is self-extinguishing acetate sheet. Cinemoid is the trade name for a range of coloured acetates 0.25mm thick which are supplied in sheets 620mm x 530mm and larger, used to colour theatrical lighting. Some suppliers can also provide coloured styrene sheet.

Extrusions

Common extrusions are formed as hollow tubes, solid circular, square and rectangular strip and some more exotic shapes such as I sections. Sizes vary from 120mm diameter plastic soil pipe in 2000mm lengths to 3mm diameter 300mm long pipe for architectural models.

Plastic conduit and trunking, used to carry electric cables, comes in a range of sizes and shapes. This includes oval, circular, square and rectangular shapes as well as bends, elbows, joints, tees and terminal boxes. Most are made of

` MY PARTNER IS NOT QUITE SURE ABOUT THE NEW KITCHEN LAYOUT! ´

PVC and you can obtain a matching solvent-weld adhesive for making joints.

Plastic sections

All materials from American sources, such as Evergreen or Plastruct, are supplied to imperial dimensions.

ABS

Strips   Columns
Angles   Rectangular tubing
Tees   Square tubing

Styrene products

White sheet   Channels
Clear sheet   I-beams
Various sizes of scale strip H-beams
V-grooved sheeting   Angles
Overlapping boards   Square tube
Corrugated metal sheet   Rectangular tube
Square tiles   Round tube
Brickwork   Half round

Figure 2.1 *The stairs and railings bring this model to life. (Photo courtesy Evergreen Scale Models)*

L section	1/32 x 1/32", 1/16 x 1/16", 3/32 x 3/32", 1/8 x 1/8", 3/16 x 3/16", 1/4 x 1/4", 5/16 x 5/16" & 3/8 x 3/8 "
H section	1/16 x 1/16", 3/32 x 3/32", 3/16 x 3/16", 1/4 x 1/4", 5/16 x 5/16" & 3/8 x 3/8"
I section	1/32 x 1/16", 3/64 x 3/32", 1/16 x 1/8", 3/32 x 3/16", 1/8 x 1/4", 5/16 x 5/32", 3/16 x 3/8", 7/32 x 7/16", 1/4 x 1/2", 1/4 x 9/16" & 1/4 x 5/8"
Round section	1/32", 1/16", 3/32", 1/8", 3/16", 1/4", 5/16" & 3/8"
Square section	1/8", 3/16", 1/4", 5/16" & 3/8"
U section	1/32 x 1/16", 3/64 x 3/32", 3/64 x 1/8", 1/16 x 3/16", 1/16 x 1/4" & 3/32 x 5/16"
Rectangular section	3/16 x 1/4", 1/4 x 5/16" & 1/4 x 3/8"
Half round section	3/16", 1/4" & 5/16"
T section	3/64 x 3/64", 1/16 x 1/16", 3/32 x 3/32", 1/8 x 1/8", 3/16 x 3/16" & 1/4 x 1/4"

Table 2.4 *The various sections and sizes of Plastruct you can buy. It is an American product produced only in imperial dimensions.*

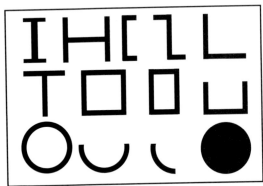

Figure 2.2 You can purchase styrene as I beams, H columns, channels, angles, tees, square, rectangular, or round tubing and clear rod.

Figure 2.3 Foam made by mixing two liquids, when it expands greatly. (Picture courtesy Deluxe Materials)

Quarter round
Round rod
Note each size of tube telescopes into the next larger size
Plasticard sheet – 355mm x 228mm (all sizes white, some sizes available in black)
0.25mm, 0.38mm, 0.50mm, 0.75mm, 1mm, 1.5mm, 2mm thick. 0.25mm clear sheet.
Plasticard sheet – 12in x 24in (305mm x 610mm)
0.25mm, 0.38mm, 0.50mm, 0.75mm, 1mm, 1.5mm and 2mm thick.
Plasticard strip – 355mm long
0.25mm, 0.40mm, 0.5mm, 0.75mm, 1mm, 1.5mm, 2mm, 2.5mm and 3.2mm thick; 0.5mm, 0.75mm, 1mm, 1.5mm, 2mm, 2.5mm, 3.2mm, 4mm, 4.8mm and 6.3mm wide.
Plasticard micro rod
0.64mm, 0.87mm, 1.2mm and 1.6mm diameter.

Other forms

Belts

A popular range of toothed belts uses metric and imperial tooth pitches from 2.5 – 10mm and 0.08in – °in. Depending on tooth pitch, widths vary from 4 – 50mm and lengths from 60 to over 4000mm.

For temperatures up to 80°C belts are made from polyurethane with steel or aramid tension members, while for temperatures up to 120°C, you should choose a polychloroprene/rubber body, reinforced with abrasion resistant polyamide or nylon fabric and using glass fibre tension members.

Poly-V, V, wedge and round belts are also made from synthetic rubber. V or wedge belts usually have specially treated sheathings to help with anti-static, oil and fire resistance. Twist link belting is made from multiple piles of reinforced polyester fabric giving low stretch, low vibration and drive tension.

Box strapping

This 12mm wide polypropylene strapping supports loads between 130kg and 200kg, depending on the grade, and is used by the packaging industry around large boxes. You can cut it to length with a sharp knife or heavy-duty scissors.

Cable ties

These ties, made from nylon, are widely used by the electronics and electrical industries to bind groups of cables together. They come either with a self-locking action once tightened or a releasable action. Popular sizes range from 2.5 – 5mm width and 110 – 340mm long and have many other uses.

Fillers

Many different fillers, most of them plastics based, are available for a wide range of modelling applications on almost any material. They range from plastic wood, a mix of sawdust in cellulose dope to today's modern micro-balloons, chemical metal and wood fillers, and epoxy putties.

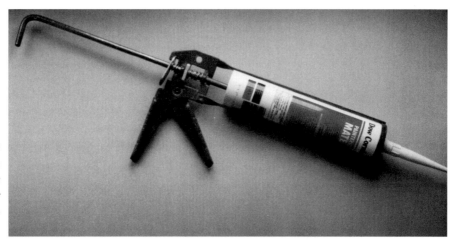

Figure 2.4 An applicator gun with a flexible acrylic filler cartridge inserted.

Foams
Some foams are sold in aerosol cans and expand when released to fill, for example, a buoyancy area in a model boat. These are fairly rigid materials and you can easily trim off any excess with a sharp knife. Other softer foams, mostly made from polyurethane, will give and are used to stuff cushions and armchairs. The foam tubing used to insulate water pipes is also widely available in a range of lengths to suit 15mm and 22mm pipes.

Grommets
Several sizes of synthetic rubber grommet are useful when building and connecting electronics, when installing R/C servos and for passing cable runs through formers and bulkheads in models using electrical power for main drive or ancillary functions. Electrical suppliers offer a range of sizes, while model shops usually carry a selection of smaller sizes.

Lubricants
Teflon- and silicone-based oils are popular lubricants with R/C car modellers and model engineers.

Silicone- and teflon-based oils
These oils work extremely well under arduous conditions and you can find them under such names as Superlube and Ultralube. Triflow with teflon is a water-displacing lubricant and is available as a liquid, grease or in an aerosol.

Moulded carvings
You can purchase small mouldings in a range of patterns and glue the small decorative plastic ones to wood or plastic surfaces to give the impression of carvings on, for example, the front of a dolls' house.

Nylon nuts and bolts
Useful when installing electronic circuit boards, nylon nuts and bolts, as well as providing insulation, also provide built-in failure at a stress level which prevents damage to the components they are joining.

Nylon is also found in Nyloc nuts to provide anti-vibration locking. Finally, nylon nuts are popular with the flying fraternity where they provide a weak link, for holding on aircraft wings, which should shear in the event of a crash.

Pipes and tubing
Low-cost, clear, flexible water pipe is generally made from PVC and has an excellent range of properties. Silicone and neoprene tubing are used to pipe fuel to internal combustion engines. For withstanding any reasonable amount of pressure, reinforced PVC will typically operate at over 10bar in sizes below 15mm.

For air lines, the choice is nylon, where even higher operating pressures are allowed. Polyurethane tubing is significantly more flexible and a very small bend radius is feasible. However, operating pressure must be limited to 5bar. You can obtain both types of tubing in pre-formed coils. In addition, reinforced PVC, neoprene or similar rubber, covered with braid reinforcement, will withstand even higher pressures.

Figure 2.5 *Ferro-plast epoxy putty turns green when the blue and yellow parts are fully mixed.*

Sealants and gasket materials

Many sealants are available from DIY stores in standard cartridges which fit into low-cost applicator guns. Sold under such names as Painters Mate, this filler is perfect for gap filling on baseboards. It is white and readily takes any sort of paint finish.

Hematite

This widely used non-hardening sticky gasket-jointing compound is used for sealing metal joints. It resists petrol, oil and diesel and withstands high pressures, steam, water and anti-freeze. It comes in a range of grades with a choice of special characteristics.

Pipe-jointing compounds

Typical of the range of compounds on the market today is one which contains PTFE and which, when applied to threaded pipes forms a flexible pressure-tight seal which resists air, oil, low pressure natural gas, steam and water. These joints are easy to dismantle when required.

Silicone rubber

This rubber is excellent as a sealant and you can also use it for making gaskets and insulating electrical items. In the electrical field, applications include sealing connectors and wire entries, as well as housings and containers.

As a single-part bath sealant, it releases acetic acid as it cures giving the characteristic smell of vinegar.

Epoxy putties

Putties are available as pairs of sticks of different colour. One is the adhesive and the other the hardener. You mix equal lengths together until you achieve an even, new third colour.

You can machine, drill and tap metal-loaded variants after they have hardened which are ideal for repairing damaged castings and even worn parts such as shafts. The metal loadings available include aluminium, bronze, steel, stainless steel and titanium.

Potting compounds

Encapsulating electronic components is done to protect them from the environment, which may be oil and vibration in models powered by internal combustion engines, damp in the case of sailing boats, or just dust in the case of model railways.

Epoxy

Where a hard exterior is required, epoxy is the right choice. Two parts, comprising resin and hardener are premixed before pouring and thermally conductive variants are available to remove heat from hot-spots.

Polyurethane

This material is available as a two-part flexible encapsulant which does not give off heat during the curing process and protects delicate electronics from moisture, water ingress and vibration. A variant allows the easy removal of the cured material should a unit prove defective or fail at a later date, while another is semi-rigid, optically clear and often used for decorative purposes.

Silicone rubber

Transparent and opaque silicone materials provide excellent mechanical support for electronic components as well as keeping dampness at bay.

Fabrics, cords and threads

Nylon and polyester (terylene) woven materials come in a range of sizes and weights. More stretch resistant composite polyester materials are mylar or melinex, which are available in weights from 10gsm upwards. You can buy all these materials off the roll in lengths to suit your needs.

Figure 2.6 Off-cuts of perspex and most other machinable plastics are available from suppliers like Proops.

Nylon, polyester and terylene threads are all popular for sewing, as well as providing rigging on model boats and aircraft. They are stronger and better able to resist a damp and/or salty atmosphere than cotton or wool.

Where to get them

There are many varied sources of plastics for modelling purposes. In some cases, you will be able to find the ready finished item in a suitable model shop. More often, you will want to purchase raw material and there are several sources, depending on what you want and whether you are prepared to accept new or second-hand material.

Yellow Pages

Plastics are readily available from suppliers around the country. Look in *Yellow Pages* for your

Art and crafts equipment/materials	Graphic-arts materials	– stockholders/suppliers
Builders' merchants	Hobby shops	– thermoforming
Chemical suppliers	Insulation materials	– vacuum forming
Containers – plastic	Jointing/gaskets	Plumbers' merchants
Dolls/dolls' houses	Model shops	Plumbing supplies
Double glazing materials	Mouldings	Polystyrene
Drawing office equipment/materials	Office stationery/supplies	Polythene suppliers
Ducting/ductwork	Pipes/fittings – flexible –	Resins
Electrical conduit	plastic	Seal manufacturers
Electronic components	Plastic encapsulation	– fluid – mechanical
Engineers' merchants/supplies	Plastics	Sealing compounds
Fishing-tackle shops	– engineering materials	Silicones
Fixings/fastenings	– fabrics, film and sheet	Synthetic resins
Foam products – latex – plastic	– laminated materials	Tapes, adhesive/industrial
Glass fibre manufacturers	– pipes/fittings	Vacuum formers

*Table 2.5 There are many headings under **Yellow Pages** for suppliers of plastic materials.*

local stockist, under the headings shown in Table 2.5, depending on exactly what you want.

Specialist suppliers

Plumbing and waste disposal uses large amounts of plastic piping, mostly PVC, of both round and square cross-section, many of which have wide applications in modelling. Diameters vary from 15mm up to 150mm and more and lengths generally start at 2000mm.

A number of model engineering suppliers hold stocks of popular plastics and these can often be found at their trade stands at modelling shows. You can buy foam sheeting and blocks of expanded polystyrene from specialist foam dealers and many street markets. Office supply and graphic-arts shops stock foam board as well as a number of different spray-on adhesives.

Model shops

Most model shops can supply materials like plasticard and styrene strip material in a variety of cross sections. Evergreen, Plastruct and Plasticard are popular names in the UK and provide a wide range of plastic materials aimed primarily at the construction of buildings, but endlessly useful for many other applications.

These shops will also carry stocks of heat-sensitive, self-adhesive films and fabrics, mainly used for covering flying model aeroplanes. You will also find they carry a wide range of plastic-based adhesives and paints. Some shops specialise, for example, in railway model supplies, but often you will find useful items which you can apply to other branches of modelling.

DIY stores

Most DIY stores sell a surprisingly wide range of plastics. These include:

- Expanded polystyrene sheet in large sizes (2400mm x 1200mm) as well as smaller fractions of this size, normally 50mm thick.
- A wide range of plastic tubing, both CPVC and UPVC, the former used for water supply; the latter for waste-water plumbing.
- Aerosol cans of foam.
- Polyester sheet.
- GRP repair kits.
- Acrylic sheet, transparent, tinted or coloured.

Figure 2.7 A range of household items provide a free source of plastic materials.

- Polycarbonate sheet. A translucent variety has insulating air channels.
- Formica-type sheet laminates.

Mail order

Mail order is an ideal way of purchasing small quantities or sizes of plastic material from the comfort of your home. Particularly with specialist materials like silicone rubber, mail order may be your only practical solution. Companies like Maplin and Electromail (the retail outlet of Radiospares), which serve the electronics market, also stock a large range of plastics in sheet and extruded form. These include many engineering plastics. Appendix A includes details of several companies which supply plastic materials.

Scrap and scrap yards

Most modellers accumulate a scrap box over a period of years. The retention of plastic offcuts and items like plastic containers, old plastic curtain rails and parts from broken domestic appliances often find practical applications. Scrap yards can be a productive source of plastics, but you will need to know what you are after.

Companies which scrap or repair photocopying machines and computer peripherals like printers and scanners are an excellent source of synthetic-rubber rollers, plastic gears and pulleys together with the appropriate belt drives.

Packaging accounts for about a third of all plastics used in the UK. From a modelling point of view, expanded polystyrene, plastic bottles and other containers, and transparent coverings are all useful. Sadly, from our point of view, improved efficiency in the packaging industry means downsizing the thickness of the materials used.

Modifying household items

There are many everyday plastic objects found around the household which you can modify for modelling use. Consider the humble one-litre plastic lemonade bottle. You can convert this to a compressed air reservoir (at not too high a pressure) for use with an airbrush, to blow water out of a submarine's ballast tanks, to raise and lower air-operated retracts on a radio controlled aircraft or even to form the basis for a model rocket.

You can cut the clear plastic material for use as a car, boat or aircraft windshield or that part of a crash helmet for a model figure or to provide other forms of glazing where the natural curvature of the material is an advantage.

Expanded polystyrene packaging is ideal for cutting to shape/size and making the hills in all types of scenic layout.

Plastics as a storage medium

The advantage of plastic containers for storage is that they do not rust and are impervious to most chemicals. Furthermore, if you choose transparent plastic, you can see inside without opening the container. In any case, indelible markers allow you to label most plastic containers.

Bags

Polythene bags are perfect for many storage and protection applications. Small, clear, self-sealing bags come in a range of sizes. They help stop you mislaying small items and also protect small part-finished or finished models. You can buy them from supermarkets and office stationery suppliers.

Boxes, drawers and racks

Whether you decide to purchase custom-built storage containers like those shown in Figure 2.8

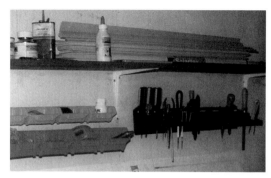

Figure 2.8 Plastic storage units and a plastic tool rack on the wall of this workshop.

or prefer to re-use commercially available items like empty ice cream or margarine containers is a matter of cost and personal preference. You can obtain commercially made, brightly-coloured polypropylene boxes with clear acrylic or translucent lids or boxes made from high-impact styrene with transparent lids.

Sets of small, clear, high-impact styrene drawers are widely available from DIY stores as well as some model shops and electronic component suppliers. They are hard wearing and perfect for storing small items.

A range of moulded plastic racks is useful for storing tools above a work surface. The plastic will not damage the sharp edges of tools and will not encourage rust.

Covers

Dust is the enemy of most modellers, and some activities generate copious quantities of dust. Polythene sheet spread over a part-built model will protect it. You can also use it to protect machine tools, but take care that the metal does not sweat and then rust beneath the cover if it is located in an area subject to wide variations in temperature and humidity – workshops in garages and sheds.

Protection

Bubble-wrap material consists of two sheets of polythene welded together with air trapped in bubbles between them. The two popular sizes of bubbles are 10mm and 25mm diameter and the main modelling use of this is for protecting delicate parts of any model during transportation.

Part 2 – Working with plastics

Health and safety

Most plastics in liquid form, and this includes many adhesives, resins and solvents, are dangerous if swallowed, inhaled or if they get into your eyes or repeated contact with your skin. Always follow the manufacturer's instructions when using them and wear disposable rubber gloves and goggles where appropriate. Keep the containers so you can read the labels and store them well out of reach of children. Good ventilation is essential when using most liquids. Unfortunately the fumes from a few of them are highly addictive. Remember that some people abuse solvents, so limit access to any you store.

Quite a few of these liquids are also highly inflammable and create toxic vapours when burned, which can cause sickness. Take care not to expose them to sparks and flames. Other plastics emit noxious fumes if burned, so again be careful, particularly during disposal. PTFE gives off poisonous fumes when set alight or even overheated (above 270°C), so extra care is needed if working with this material using machine tools.

In general, you should not think of model making with plastics as creating a serious fire risk. However, you should store solvents sensibly to avoid negating your household insurance.

Fumes from superglues are unpleasant and you should only use them in a well ventilated area. Their effect on some people appears to be cumulative to the point where the discomfort they cause makes their use impossible. Also worthy of mention is their affinity to flesh and their ability to glue your fingers, or other parts of your body, to anything and everything. Epoxy and other resins can cause or aggravate dermatitis and eczema so keep them off your skin.

When heating plastics to form them, it is important to remember how long these materials retain heat. It is sensible to wear thick protective gloves to avoid the risk of burning sensitive hands or fingers. It is also worth remembering that when thermoplastics are exposed to high temperatures they will melt and drip blobs of plastic which can cause nasty burns to the flesh or even ignite whatever they fall on.

Heat treatment of plastics brings other potential dangers. First, unpleasant fumes may be given off, so that again adequate ventilation is essential. Second, some plastics are more readily inflammable than others. Thus facilities for smothering any accidental fire are crucial. Even cutting plastics like styrene with a power saw may be hazardous as the heat from the blade tends to melt the plastic and jam the blade.

Some of the more brittle plastics will shatter if over-enthusiastically worked, so it is a good idea to wear safety glasses or goggles to protect the eyes. Sanding most plastics produces an unpleasant dust, which you should not inhale. This is also true of the dust from the fibres used in composite materials. Avoid inhaling dust when sanding any plastic and take particular care with fillers and hardened mixes containing microballoons. A protective mask is a must if you are creating any significant amount of dust.

Working with GRP and silicone rubber

Working with GRP is safe providing you take some simple precautions and handle the materials with care. Always follow the manufacturer's instructions and only let children work with GRP under adult supervision.

The catalysts are inflammable and will attack your skin, eyes and mouth. If you get catalyst on your skin quickly wash it off. If in your eyes, rinse them under running water for 15 minutes and seek immediate medical attention. Polyester resin emits inflammable vapours which you should not inhale. The acetone for cleaning brushes is also inflammable. Do not smoke and make sure you work in a well ventilated area. Safely store materials when not in use. Silicone rubber constituents have similar dangers.

Use rubber or plastic gloves and a barrier cream. These gloves provide perfect protection when working with the constituent parts of materials like GRP and silicone rubber. They are usually made of latex or PVC and come in a range of sizes. Economical to purchase in quantities, you can discard them after each working session.

Storage of plastics

Some materials, like polyester resin, silicone rubber, their catalysts and instant (cyanoacrylate) glues have quite short shelf lives; months not years. You can usually extend the shelf life by refrigeration or freezing. Read the manufacturer's instructions to find the best way to store any particular material.

Storage of plastic sheet and rod should follow normal practice for storing wood. In both forms, plastics will warp if not stored either flat or vertically. Odd scraps may obviously live in a suitable box, but avoid mixing soft plastics like foams or expanded polystyrene with harder materials due to the risk of damage to the former.

Disposal

Many plastics burn readily, producing lots of smoke and sometimes toxic gases. PVC when burned, for example, produces hydrochloric acid! Polythene and polystyrene have three times the calorific value of wood.

Most plastics made to date have not been bio-degradable. Recent developments have included some plastics which do slowly degrade under the influence of low levels of ultra-violet light for use in agriculture and for protecting car finishes during manufacture. However, the majority of applications demand exactly the opposite qualities and these are the materials we are likely to encounter. Therefore, dispose of any scrap plastic in your rubbish bin or take it to the local tip, rather than trying to burn it.

I THINK THE FOG OF WAR ADDS TO THE REALISM ... AND IT GETS RID OF ALL MY SCRAP PLASTIC!

Chapter 3 Working plastics with hand and power tools

Hand working plastics

You can work plastics with wood or metal working tools, some of which may need special preparation in terms of the way you sharpen them. When drilling or sawing, you must support the material underneath the cutting area.

The key to success is to make haste slowly as it is easy to overheat plastics when sawing or drilling them. They will then start to melt, stick to the cutting tool and ruin the cut.

For many tasks, hand tools are better than powered ones as it is much easier to control the heat generated at the cutting surface.

Bending

While most plastic materials will bend relatively easily, they will also spring back to their original shape once you release the force bending them, unless you have exceeded their elastic limit. You can usually observe this point by bending a piece of the plastic until it starts to go white at the bend, indicating you have reached the limit. Permanent deformation is simple with thermoplastics by heating the material while it is bent. Of course this is not possible with thermosetting materials. There is much more information about the use of heat to form plastics in Chapter 5.

Cutting

There are several alternative ways of cutting plastics, the choice of tool depending on the type and thickness of the plastic as well as the straightness or curve of the cut. You can use a knife, scissors, a saw or a nibbler.

Knives

A knife and a metal ruler is the preferred cutting method if you want a straight line. This method works on softer plastics up to 3mm thick.

Figure 3.1 You can achieve a lot with a craft knife, hand drill and selection of files.

A self-healing cutting mat, commercially available in a range of sizes and made from three layers of polyvinyl, will protect the surface beneath. Figure 3.2 illustrates cutting on one of these mats.

An easy way of cutting most plastic sheet materials is to score a line along one surface. Then place the scored line over the edge of your work surface and bend along the line until the plastic snaps. This should result in a clean break. Thicker materials may require several passes of a sharp knife. For fast, clean and accurate cutting of styrene shapes, tubing, strip and rod, simply scribe with a craft knife and snap.

Scissors

All the thin plastic sheet materials, such as nylon, polyester and polythene fabrics or films as well as many of the softer sheets up to 1.5mm thick, are readily cut with a pair of sharp scissors. This is particularly useful where an irregular shape is required. For thicker materials you can employ tin shears which will make short work of the tougher cut.

Saws and nibblers

You can hand saw almost any thick rigid plastic as long as the saw blade is not too fine. A hacksaw is probably the ideal type of saw for this purpose, though for cutting smaller items, a razor saw is preferable. It is important to control the rate of sawing as, if too fast, you will overheat the plastic and spoil the line of the cut as well as clog the saw. Use a hacksaw blade with around five teeth per centimetre.

Nibblers are one of the best tools for cutting rigid thermoset plastics like formica.

Removing material

There are many ways of shaping a piece of plastic and, as with other materials, you can sand, file, scrape or plane it to the size you want.

Sanding

Sanding any plastic is best done with a wet and dry emery paper or silicon carbide paper. This will reduce the heat imparted by the abrasive process and help to stop clogging by the plastic dust resulting from the sanding action. A relatively fine paper, not worked too fast, and preferably a wet and dry paper worked wet is the best way of finishing off plastic which you have cut to size.

If the quality of the finish is important, work with increasingly fine grades of emery paper and finish off with a polish. If, on the other hand, you wish to simulate a wood surface, say on styrene sheet, then rubbing it with coarse sandpaper will produce a realistic effect.

Filing

A fairly coarse file and a relatively slow speed is the key to removing material. You can then use a

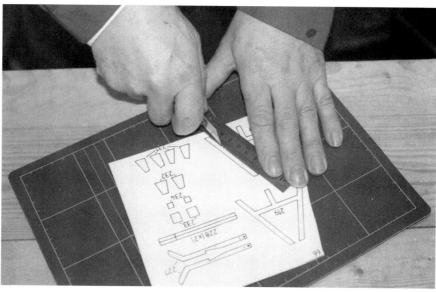

Figure 3.2 Thin plastic sheet is easily cut with a sharp craft knife. The mat protects the work surface below.

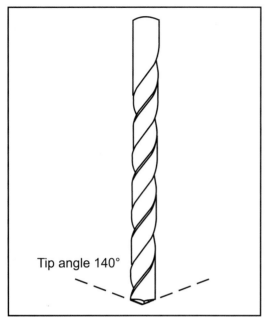

Tip angle 140°

Figure 3.3 *The tip of a drill for use on plastics should be ground to an angle of 140°.*

fine file to smooth the final surface finish, unless you purposely require a rough finish.

Scraping

Probably the best way of finishing flat edges of stiff plastic sheet is with a square-edged steel scraper or a craft knife blade held at right angles to the edge. With practice, this will produce a beautifully smooth result.

Planing

You can use a plane on some plastics, both to remove material and to improve the finish of the cut material. Take care, however, only to take a fairly shallow cut to avoid the plane digging in. You can also use a Surform plane on rigid plastics.

Polishing

You should remove deep scratches with a scraper before rubbing down with increasingly fine wet and dry paper. Polishing plastics which you have worked is a straightforward if painstaking task. A metal polish, such as Brasso, has mildly abrasive properties and you can use it to produce a gleaming finish. Alternatively, you can try a gentle abrasive like kieselguhr or rouge.

Drilling and thread cutting

As with sawing, a slow speed is essential to avoid overheating, making a hand drill a useful tool in this context. Figure 3.3 shows the ideal shape for the drill tip. If you have a grindstone, try shaping the tip to this profile.

To cut threads, the use of taps and dies with coarse threads is usually best. Because plastics give, tapped threads will be a tight fit. Like drilled holes, they tend to be undersize. You should only use self-tapping screws in non-brittle plastics where the thread can bite. Where components will be subject to stress, it is best not to put a thread in the plastic but to fit a threaded metal insert.

Using power tools

It is a generalisation, but the types of plastic you may wish to machine and their final use tend to be very different from those which you work by hand. You can mostly machine plastics using the techniques recommended for working with aluminium, though the machining properties of plastics do vary from type to type.

The most important single issue is to **avoid any overheating of the material** during the machining process. Once the plastic starts to soften, it will adhere to the tool and/or the material itself, increasing friction and adding to the over-heating problem. Some thermoplastics start to soften at around 100°C and this temperature is quickly reached at the cutting edge of the tool, particularly because of the low thermal conductivity of plastics.

Swarf should cut cleanly and be crisp; overheating makes it soft and blurred. Tools must be sharp and smooth. The use of a coolant to protect the material, rather than the tool, is all but essential. A test is a good idea as some soluble oils will craze certain plastics, but soapy water is suitable for all these materials. Ensure the plastic is held securely and, if necessary, support it so that it cannot flex.

Cutting edges should have little or no rake, or even a small amount of negative rake. Back clearance is essential. Plastics, especially some of the filled ones soon blunt tools, so that HSS is recommended. Swarf tends to cling due to the build up of static, though some forms of anti-static plastic are available. This also applies when using hand tools.

Cutting

While it is usually easy to cut relatively thin plastic sheet with a craft or Stanley knife, both office and workshop guillotines will cleanly cut thin sheet plastic material. For thicker materials, power tools can simplify the task.

All power saws tend to overheat plastics. The rate of feed and speed of cut are critical and are best judged from experience. At all times support the work to avoid chatter. Tallow is a suitable lubricant for all blades, but remember that very fine-toothed blades tend to clog.

Band saws

For an average thickness of material, use a blade with 5 teeth per centimetre (12 per inch). For thicker grades, those with 2 teeth per centimetre (5 per inch) may perform better. Widely spaced teeth help to stop clogging. In all cases, adjust the saw guides to a close fit to minimise any tendency for the cut to wander.

Circular saws

For cutting plastics, the teeth must run true. The tip of each tooth should touch an imaginary circle as any tooth projecting can cause splintering. True up any irregularity by carefully grinding the blade on the machine itself.

For general cutting, you should use negative rake and slight forward set. Saws with a pitch of 3 teeth per centimetre (8 per inch) suit most plastics, but those with 2 teeth per centimetre (5 per inch) are better suited to thick sections. Swarf is cleared more easily if the base of each tooth is rounded. The best is a hollow ground blade which is not in contact behind the cutting edge. You can minimise the risk of chipping by attaching adhesive tape to each side of the cutting line.

You can purchase blades specially designed to cut non-ferrous metals and plastics. They perform best when coated with oil or wax prior to use. You can also obtain similar blades with carbide-tipped teeth and covered with a non-stick coating.

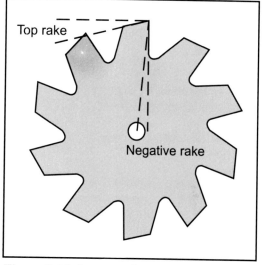

Figure 3.4 *It is essential to set the correct rake for sawing plastic materials.*

Jig saws

If you use a jig saw, you can buy blades specially designed for cutting plastics. Otherwise a blade with about 5 – 8 teeth per centimetre (12 – 20 per inch) is suitable. Again, move the saw slowly to stop any overheating.

Laminate trimmers

You can readily cut irregular shapes in some of the harder plastic, such as formica, using a specially designed power laminate trimmer. These tools are particularly useful for cutting irregular shapes.

Drilling

For soft plastics, drills with a slow spiral or helix angle and smooth wide flutes are the best. For all work, the angle of the point should be obtuse – up to 140°. This increases its slicing action and is particularly important when drilling thin sheets because of the risk that the cutting point will pierce the sheet before the whole cutting edge of the drill is in contact. As with sheet metal, this can result in tearing. Keep both the drill speed and the feed rate to a minimum.

Holes drilled in most plastics end up slightly undersize because the material gives under the cutting pressure. This accounts for the tight fit of a drill in its hole and allows the shank of the drill

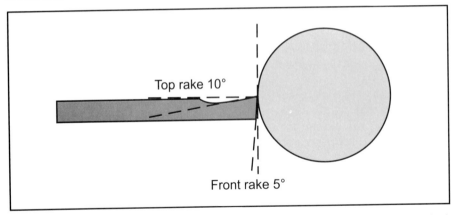

Figure 3.5 Grind any tool, used for cutting plastic in the lathe, to give the correct front and top rakes.

to be in rubbing contact with the sides of the hole. To avoid friction, consider grinding back the lands beyond the first 10mm. Alternatively, grind the point to a slightly off-centre chisel edge. This makes the drill cut slightly oversize.

Turning

You can turn plastics in a lathe in much the same way as metals. However, unlike turning metal, where you are careful not to overheat the tip of the tool, with plastics it is the material you are cutting which is at risk of damage. Slow speeds are essential to avoid overheating the plastic and softening it so that it sticks to the cutting tool. It should also be clear from Chapter 1 that only certain plastics are suitable for machining.

Particularly good are acetal, delrin, a range of nylons, perspex, torlon, tufnol, tufset and vitrex. As an example, the cutting speed for tufnol should be roughly the same as for aluminium.

Tools

A good cutting edge to a lathe tool is essential. For average work, 5° to 10° of top rake is suggested. At least 5° front rake is necessary to avoid overheating. This angle should not be too great, however, or the tool will soon blunt. Inadequate top rake often causes splintering.

Milling and routing

Cutters with up to 10° positive front rake and 20° top rake are suitable for milling plastics. For routing, normal high-speed woodworking tools

Figure 3.6 You can still use conventional metal working machine tools like a lathe or milling machine to work plastics.

are most suitable. You can use any type of cutter, single or double edged, but you should grind a slight angle for back clearance. Routing is not a practical proposition for thermoplastics due to the high speed of the routing tool melting the plastic. It is, however, a completely different matter for thermosetting plastics. Formica, for example, is often routed to shape before it is applied to a kitchen.

Sanding

Sanding is best done by hand, with a wet and dry emery paper used wet, as power sanders generate sufficient heat to soften or melt the plastic, ruining the workpiece.

Polishing

Polishing plastics with a power tool requires care to avoid overheating. You should use a pad filled with a buffing compound and use a light touch and the lowest speed you can. You must first cut back deep scratches with emery or a scraper before rubbing down with graded abrasives. You can bring dull surfaces to a high gloss with a calico buffing wheel and a gentle abrasive such as rouge or kieselguhr. Remember that blemishes in highly polished materials, such as perspex, are very noticeable and are magnified by refraction.

Finishing models

Etchants

The smooth finish of many plastic materials provides little grip for some adhesives and paints. The use of an etchant, as well as cleaning the

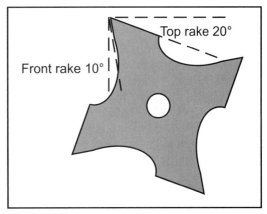

Figure 3.7 It is essential to get the correct top rake on any mill.

surface of the plastic, will provide a better surface for the adhesive to adhere. Prymol is an etchant that has been specially developed for use with the range of covering materials made by Solarfilm and prevents overlapping film materials becoming loose.

Solvents

Acetone

Acetone is ideal for cleaning brushes which have been used with cellulose paint or polyester resin. You can also use it for cleaning printed circuit boards to remove the flux. Take care as it has a low flash point and will dissolve many plastics.

Cellulose thinners

Less expensive than acetone, you can use thinners in the same way to clean brushes after painting with cellulose or working with GRP resin.

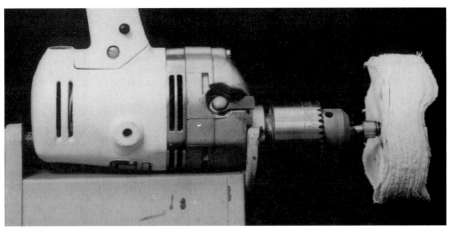

Figure 3.8 A buffing mop fitted to a standard hand-held drill helps to get that final polish on any plastic item. (Photo courtesy Alec Tiranti)

Cleaners

Take care when using some cleaners as they may affect certain plastics. Cleaners are generally safe on thermosetting plastics but may damage acrylics and polystyrene. Water-based aqueous cleaners are a good alternative if you have any doubts or have tried a test sample and found that a solvent attacks it.

Anti-static

Static causes problems for many modellers, particularly those working with plastic materials which are such poor conductors. Prime of these are the difficulties when working with sensitive electronics like CMOS components. However, static can cause difficulties for anyone trying to polish any transparent item, such as a model windscreen or canopy, not to mention a display cabinet or a clock dome.

You can purchase anti-static cleaners and treatments in aerosols, bottles and pump/spray containers. These cleaners are also ideal for use on computer screens. The ones designed for use in electronics assembly areas are specially long lasting.

Tack cloths

These dust-retaining cloths are ideal for wiping down the surface of models prior to painting. Made from viscose rayon, a cellulose-based product, they pick up particles of dust from the surface of a model and retain them within their fibres.

Dopes, paints and varnishes

Polyurethane paints and varnishes used to be the market leaders for durability but are seriously challenged by acrylic-based paints, which allow you to clean your brushes with water. There are epoxy resin based two-part paints which are very durable and resist attack from most fuels. There are also two-part fuel proofers suitable for use on internal-combustion engine powered models. Cellulose dope in clear and coloured form has been the traditional paint of aeromodellers, but coloured dope is now rarely used, unless sprayed, due to the difficulty in achieving a good finish with a paint brush.

It is essential to recognise which types of paint are safe for which plastic. Most will accept acrylic or enamel paints without detrimental effects. Cellulose paint, normally sold in aerosol cans to repair damage on your car, attacks styrene plastics, but is safe on ABS.

Not all paints are compatible and the wrong combination will result in paint bubbling and a ruined finish. Basically, never put cellulose on top of enamel. If you are in any doubt about compatibility, try a test sample first. Remember that most paints take time to harden completely, so be patient between coats.

Acrylics

Although water-based, manufacturers usually recommend that you thin acrylic paints with methylated spirits. Acrylic varnishes provide a

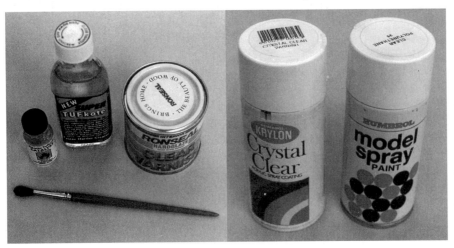

Figure 3.9 Paints and varnishes may be one or two-part and come in brushable form or in ready-to-spray aerosol cans.

tough, non-yellowing finish. Acrylics are quick drying and resistant to boiling water and alcohol. They are non-inflammable, non-toxic and virtually smell free. You can clean brushes in water. The wide range of colours on the market is becoming increasingly popular.

Celluloses

Dope, or more properly cellulose dope, was traditionally used in the aircraft industry in the first half of the twentieth century to shrink the covering material, make it airtight and provide the final colour scheme. As a result, it was also widely used by aeromodellers for the same purpose. It was, and still is, used by the motor car industry, although cellulose paints are increasingly being replaced by water-based acrylic paints covered with a protective varnish. The wide availability of an enormous range of colours in handy aerosol cans is a boon for modellers, though care is required when you use these sprays.

You need good ventilation and an area where excess paint spray will not cause damage. For small items, a cardboard box, open on one side, is portable and perfect for spraying. You should invest in a simple face mask to avoid inhaling paint. Ensure the item you are painting is perfectly clean. Shake the aerosol so the bead inside rattles to mix the paint for the specified time, usually two minutes. Then spray a light coat from a distance of 250 – 300 mm, keeping the spray continuously moving. The secret is to put on many light coats to avoid sags in the paint. This is not a problem as cellulose paint is very rapid drying.

Enamels

For painting most models, enamel paints are unbeatable. Matt enamels have superb covering powers, though you must protect them with a coat of lacquer or varnish if you are going to handle them afterwards. They provide excellent results even when applied with a brush and Humbrol offers a huge range of colours, with the more popular ones in aerosol spray cans as well as tins.

Epoxies

Specialist two-part cold-cure plastic coatings are available for use on wood, cork and plastic laminates. They are clear liquids which do not discolour or darken with age. They adhere strongly, can be burnished to a mirror finish or rubbed down with steel wool and wax to give a satin finish. Both finishes are resistant to heat, water, solvents and abrasion.

Polyurethanes

Paints and varnishes based on polyurethane have a reputation as hard wearing. The varnishes do exhibit some yellowing with age and exposure to sunlight and you need to clean brushes with white spirit.

Self-adhesive sheeting and strips

Many models can have their final decoration applied in the form of plastic self-adhesive strip or sheet, usually vinyl sheet. This is treated with a pressure-sensitive adhesive which will stick to most materials once the protective backing is removed.

There is a range of coloured velours, useful for lining display cases and storage boxes, as well as plain coloured sheets, including many different simulated leather and wood grain finishes. Take care not to trap air bubbles under the surface of the sheeting. Apply it from one edge and gently press across the sheet from that edge. If you do get an air bubble, pricking it with a fine needle

Figure 3.10 There is a very wide choice of self-adhesive plastic decorative sheeting.

will usually allow you to smooth out the bubble without any sign of damage.

Self-adhesive decorative vinyl strips are supplied in rolls of varying widths from as thin as 1mm and in a variety of colours. To apply them, cut a suitable length, peel away the backing material and carefully press down in place.

Decals

Originally referred to as transfers in the UK, the North American term decal has found wide acceptance and is used throughout this book. Typically decals need soaking in warm water for about a quarter to half a minute before you apply them to your model. You may find a wetting agent, such as Micro Sol added to the warm water helps avoid bubbles of air getting trapped under the decal and improves adhesion. For decals on compound curves, a stretching agent like Micro Set will help the decal conform to the surface beneath.

Lettering

Self-adhesive lettering and other forms of numeric or written decoration are found in three different forms. There is self-adhesive vinyl sheeting, rub-down lettering and the traditional decals. Vinyl sheet is comparatively thick compared with the other two, making it less suitable for small models. You will find many popular typefaces in stationery and graphic arts shops. You will also find rub-down lettering.

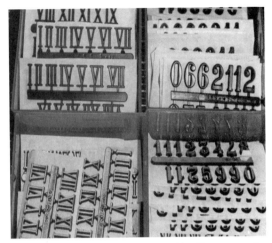

Figure 3.11 *A selection of self-adhesive polyvinyl numbers.*

For clock makers there is quite a range of brass finished polyvinyl Roman and Arabic numerals with self-adhesive backs which may suit some specialist requirements.

Dyeing

You can only dye some plastics but nylon is easily coloured by this method using a small packet of dye, readily available from hardware stores. Other materials which are fairly easy to dye include expanded polystyrene and cellulose acetate. As usual, if in doubt, try a test with a small sample.

'DINNER'S READY, DEAR'

Chapter 4 Joining plastics to themselves and other materials

The choice of adhesives

Many plastics are notoriously difficult to glue making it hard to select the best adhesive, from the many on the market, for joining various plastics to themselves and other materials. A review of the main groups of adhesives shows their strengths and weaknesses and highlights their main uses. Specialist adhesives are regularly appearing on the market with improved or new characteristics. Those covered in this chapter are those available at the beginning of 1998.

Adhesives are broadly classified as natural or synthetic. Natural sources include those obtained from animals, vegetables and minerals and are only referred to if they are useful for gluing plastics. The ones which are synthetically derived are plastics and group into:

• Synthetic rubbers and their derivatives.

• Thermoplastics.
• Thermosetting plastics.

The way in which adhesives work varies and can broadly be grouped into a number of categories. Their method of working does influence their use:

1. Solvent/water evaporation or absorption.
2. Hot melt.
3. Heat or pressure sensitive.
4. Chemical setting – polyester and epoxy resins, silicone rubber.

There are several factors which you should consider when selecting an adhesive for a particular job:

• The materials you wish to join.
• The type of joint you are making.
• How long you are prepared to wait for the join to set.

Figure 4.1 The range of modellers' glues made by just one company. (Photo courtesy Deluxe Materials)

- The conditions the joint will endure.
- The strength and permanence of the joint.
- Any need for initial tack.
- The colour of the adhesive when set.
- The pot and shelf lives of the adhesive.
- The inflammability, smell and toxicity of the adhesive.
- The cost of the adhesive.

You may also wish to think about the form of the adhesive – liquid, paste, film, powder – whether it is solvent- or water-based and how you will apply it. You may be able to apply the glue directly from the tube, using a spreader or spatula or even straight from an aerosol can. Some adhesives are two part and you must mix them in the correct proportions before use, while others work by applying one part to one surface and the other to the second and then bringing the two surfaces together.

Remember that most, but not all, adhesives depend for their adhesion on perfectly clean surfaces. This can be a special problem with plastics and metals, where even the oils from your skin can prevent a successful joint. For the best joints, always roughen the surface with sandpaper and then clean with a solvent to remove any oil or grease. If you are in any doubt about solvent compatibility with your plastic, you can always use soapy water. From the modeller's point of view, the key factors for any adhesive are strength and cost, and these are shown in Table 4.1 for a range of popular glues.

The bond with some materials is strong, with others it is weak. Some materials cannot be glued together at all. The effectiveness of an adhesive depends on factors like the temperature, porosity of the surfaces, their fit and the load the joint will experience. Table 4.2 lists some suitable adhesives for bonding different materials together. Nylon, polycarbonate and polythene are particularly difficult to glue and it is only with recent formulations that you can obtain any degree of success.

There is an useful book called **Adhesives and Sealants** by Dave Lammas (Workshop Practice Series No 21). It gives a thorough grounding for anyone wishing to gain an in-depth understanding of the subject of adhesives.

Acrylic

These glues are often the only ones which will bond some awkward materials and provide an immensely strong bond. The list includes acrylic, ABS, epoxy, GRP, both epoxy- and polyester-based, metal, polyester, PVC and wood. The adhesive is made up by dissolving a powder in a liquid until it thickens after some 5 – 10 minutes (Deluxe Materials Fusion) or mixing a powder into a jelly (Pattex Stabilit Express).

	Cost	Gap filling	Drying time	Penetration	Strength	Weight
Acrylic	High	Good	Med	Poor	High	Med
Aliphatic	Low	Poor	Med	Good	Med	Med
Contact	Med	Poor	Med	V poor	High	Med
Cyano	High	Poor	V fast	V good	Med	V low
Epoxy	High	Good	Med/slow	Poor	V high	High
Hot glue	Med	Good	Fast	V poor	Med	High
Polyester resin	Med	Good	Slow	Med	High	High
PVA	Low	Med	Slow	Med	Med	Med
Solvent weld	Med	V poor	Fast	Good	Med	V low

Table 4.1 The main characteristics of the adhesives used for gluing plastics to themselves and a wide range of other modelling materials.

	Paper	Wood	Metal	ABS	Acrylic	Acetate
Acrylic		✓		✓	✓	
Aliphatic	✓	✓				
Contact	✓	✓	✓			
Cyano		✓	✓	✓		✓
Epoxy	✓	✓	✓			
Hot glue		✓	✓			
Polyester resin	✓	✓	✓		✓	
PVA	✓	✓				✓
Solvent/cement				✓	✓	✓
	Foam	Formaldehyde	GRP	Nylon	Phenolic	Polycarb'
Acrylic			✓	✓		✓
Aliphatic	✓					
Contact	Some	✓			✓	
Cyano		✓	✓			
Epoxy		✓	✓			
Hot glue						
Polyester resin			✓			
PVA	✓					
Solvent/cement						
	Polyester	Polypropylene	Poly-thene	Poly-styrene	PVC	Synthetic rubber
Acrylic	✓				✓	
Aliphatic						
Contact					✓	✓
Cyano		✓	✓		✓	✓
Epoxy				✓		
Hot glue		✓	✓	✓		
Polyester resin					✓	
PVA					✓	
Solvent/cement				✓	✓	

Table 4.2 *Always use the right adhesive for gluing plastics to themselves and other modelling materials.*

These glues have good filling properties but must be left to set, providing a strong joint within about an hour. Except for a specialist glue like Deluxe Materials Super Crylic, the materials you are joining must be clean and grease free. These adhesives will not bond to polythene or PTFE.

Fast-acting variants cure in about one minute and are two-part adhesives. You have to apply the glue to one surface and the activator to the other prior to bringing the parts together for a rapid and permanent bond.

Aliphatic

Aliphatic resin glue is a waterproof, yellow glue for joining wood, including balsa, which dries faster, provides a stronger bond and is easier to sand than PVA white glue. It results in a slightly less flexible joint than PVA, but is relatively light-weight after drying out.

Penetrating aliphatics now allow you to assemble wooden joints, and some plastic ones, prior to the application of the glue, which will then penetrate the joint in the same way as cyano.

Anaerobic

Anaerobic adhesives are single component liquids which cure in the absence of air and the famous brand name Loctite is often used generically to describe this type of adhesive. Different grades are available for thread locking and metal retaining applications:

- Low strength where you may want to undo or adjust the fastener at a later stage.
- Medium strength to prevent the fastener vibrating loose.
- Medium strength for retaining bearings, bushes and oil seals.
- High strength for retaining close fitting and press-fit parts after assembly.
- High strength for permanent locking of studs and other parts which you never wish to disassemble.

Cement

In this case, we are not talking about the grey powder, mixed with sand for building construction! Of the range of cements on the market, balsa cement is one of the best known and is a cellulose-based glue which is ideal, as its name suggests, for joining pieces of balsa wood to each other.

Solvent cements are suspensions of small particles of plastic in a suitable solvent. PVC and polystyrene cements are useful for joining these thermoplastics, though some produce quite toxic vapours. Thus good ventilation is essential when working with them.

Figure 4.2 Acrylic two-part glues are ideal for joining formers to GRP. (Photo courtesy Deluxe Materials)

Contact glue

Contact adhesives are designed to be spread on each surface and left to dry. The two surfaces are then carefully brought together to give an instant bond. For gluing sheet materials and laminates such as formica, they are ideal.

A specialist requirement of modellers is to bond wood veneer to expanded polystyrene foam. This calls for a liquid synthetic rubber (usually polychloroprene) or latex-based glue, as many contact adhesives use a petroleum-based solvent which will simply dissolve the polystyrene. Petroleum-based glues are becoming rarer as users demand solvent-free adhesives.

Some of these glues, such as Copydex, are pure white and dry to a near transparent yellow, while others such as Aero Bond are coloured so you can see where you have applied them. These glues are also ideal for joining fabric materials both to themselves and to wood or plastic.

Cyano

Cyanoacrylates, or superglues are almost weightless and provide a solid bond in seconds. They come in a range of viscosities including thixotropic. The thinner ones are particularly well suited to joining balsa wood. You can use the thicker ones on porous materials or on vertical surfaces. Some special variants have been developed to work on polythene, polypropylene and expanded polystyrene.

An activating spray is particularly useful when working with plastics as it allows the glue to bond to many different types of plastic. It is applied to one surface, the cyano to the other and allows

you to bring the surfaces together for an instant bond. Alternatively, you can apply the activator after gluing the joint. Fillers enable you to form a fillet with these glues.

Store unopened bottles in cool dark conditions. The fridge is ideal. Once opened, keep the lid on when not in use but do not refrigerate as taking the bottle in and out of the fridge promotes condensation which will quickly make the glue unusable. Also, never forget that cyano bonds the skin and you should take care to keep it off your fingers, and any other exposed skin. A debonder will release bonded skin and many other joined materials, but attacks acrylics and polystyrene.

Epoxy

Epoxy resins form one of the strongest class of adhesives. They are two-part glues which require careful mixing in the proportions specified on the container, usually 1:1. Setting times vary from a few minutes, usually five, through one hour to

Figure 4.3 Veneer is usually attached to the expanded polystyrene foam core of a wing with a coloured polychloroprene or latex-based glue.

Figure 4.4 Roket powder helps fill gaps when using low viscosity cyano. (Photo courtesy Deluxe Materials)

twenty-four hours. The longer the setting time, generally, the stronger the bond. Bonding times are quoted for normal temperatures. All epoxies give off heat when curing and should therefore only be mixed in small quantities. You can accelerate setting and improve the strength of the joint by warming it with a hot-air gun or by placing the joint on a radiator or even in a cool oven, provided the materials you are bonding will withstand the heat. Heat-resistant epoxies will work without failing at somewhat higher temperatures than normal epoxies and, as they will also resist hot exhaust fuel and oil, you may judiciously use them on exhaust systems. Epoxies are excellent gap-fillers and provide exceptional strength when joining metals.

However, epoxy joints will fail unless the materials you are joining are clean and perfectly grease free, and this includes the grease contained in finger marks. Epoxies are heavy because the bond is caused by chemical reaction rather than solvent evaporation. Epoxies are not recommended for use with thermoplastics but will bond to ceramics, glass, jewellery, leather, metal, rubber, stone and most hard thermosetting plastics. They have virtually no shrinkage and can be formed into small components in a plasticine mould. Alternatively, you can use a two-part epoxy putty for this task or as a permanent filler. You can remove excess or spilled epoxy before it has set with white spirit. Epoxies which are silver loaded

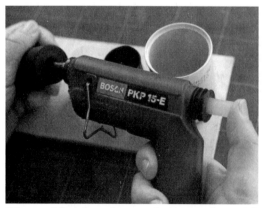

Figure 4.5 A hot-glue gun being used to stick plastic containers to a plywood base.

are good as an occasional substitute for soldered joints.

Epoxy resins are used for making high quality composite materials, particularly those based on carbon fibre and Kevlar. They provide better impact resistance than composites made with polyester resin.

Hot glue

Hot glue is not a single type of adhesive since a range of materials is available in the form of glue sticks which you can feed into a hot-glue gun. All-purpose sticks are colourless and will join materials such as brick, fabric, leather, metal, PVC, tiles and wood.

These glues only work with joints which will not be exposed to heat and where the heat of the glue will not damage the materials you are joining. They have excellent gap-filling capabilities and you can trim off excess glue with a sharp knife after it has cooled.

Coloured glue sticks, sticks with varying set times, heat resistance and viscosities are all available. Some hot glue variants will stick to polythene and polypropylene, while low melt ones are suitable for bonding board, fabric, film, polystyrene and plastic foams as well as wood.

Polyester

Polyester resins are normally used as the plastic part of glass reinforced plastic (GRP). They are, however, also useful for gluing metal or wooden parts to completed GRP items. Good examples include the placing of formers, rudder post and prop shaft in a GRP boat hull and the lead shot weights in a yacht's fin.

PVA

This white woodworkers' glue is widely sold both by DIY stores and model shops. It is ideal for joining wood and comes in water soluble and waterproof forms. It provides a slightly flexible joint which can prove difficult to sand. Standard variants take about 30 minutes to provide an initial grip, but there are several variants which only take around 10 minutes. Some brands dry completely transparent.

For building models, avoid the cheaper brands in DIY stores as they often contain additional fillers which reduce the strength of the subsequent joint.

Urea formaldehyde

Aerolite 306 is a woodworking glue which is also ideal for bonding laminated plastics, like formica, to wood. A two-part glue, one part is applied to each surface and the two parts then brought together to provide a strong heat and waterproof joint.

General-purpose and specialist glues

There are several specialist and general-purpose glues such as glass bond, vinyl bond, clear glue and GP adhesive which are useful for particular applications. The manufacturer's instructions, or the name of the glue will guide you in terms of what materials they will join.

Aerosol spray cans of fixing glues

Cans of spray mount, used to attach card, paper and film during the preparation of artwork, also find a number of modelling applications. Typical is the attachment of a background or sky scene on a small gauge model railway.

Welding plastics with heat or solvents

You can weld any thermoplastic by careful application of heat. You do, however, need to take care not to melt the materials you are trying to join. A soldering iron with a clean tip is an excellent welding tool as is a knife blade heated in a flame.

You can also join thermoplastics with a suitable solvent. The disadvantage of pure solvents is that they have no gap-filling capability as they totally evaporate. The ideal solvent is one which dissolves rapidly and evaporates quickly so that the surfaces are attacked for the shortest time possible. However, the action must not be so rapid that you cannot make the join properly before the surfaces have dried.

Any trace of solvent, even the solvent vapour, can cause crazing and produce an unsightly blemish. You should mask the area around any join to avoid spoiling it. Masking tape is suitable as it does not affect the material itself. To place the solvent accurately, you can use a small paint brush or hypodermic syringe.

Solvent cements act fast and you may have difficulty covering a large area before they have evaporated. The formation of a skin will indicate a weakening in any resulting join.

Chloroform

This colourless liquid was historically used for joining perspex by applying the chloroform to the

THE INSTRUCTIONS SAID JUST WELD TWO ITEMS TOGETHER!

joint with a small paint brush, which would then flow into the join and take about an hour to set.

Chloroform is also an anaesthetic which will send you to sleep, so you had to work in a well-ventilated area. However, it is increasingly difficult to obtain and you will have to sign a register for it at a pharmacist. A better and safer alternative is a clear acrylic glue like Deluxe Materials Fusion.

Methyl ethyl ketone (MEK)

MEK is a widely used plastic solvent which will work with many thermoplastics including styrene sheet and strip, where its application is widespread.

Micro Weld, Plastic Magic and Plastic Weld

You can join styrene and ABS with Micro Weld, Plastic Magic or Plastic Weld, which are clear, liquid solvents which set in minutes and bond permanently overnight. They dissolve a thin layer of each surface, evaporate quickly, and form a joint as strong as the surrounding plastic.

Tapes

Insulating tape

As well as normal PVC insulating tape, which comes in a range of colours and widths, there is a yellow polyester equivalent which has excellent mechanical and electrical properties as well as good abrasion and heat resistance.

As temperatures rise, a polyimide-based tape with a silicone thermosetting adhesive will provide better protection, while glass tape with a similar adhesive withstands continuous exposure to 180°C and occasional exposure to 250°C.

Self-amalgamating tape

When stretched as they are wrapped around cables, joints or pipes, these tapes will gradually amalgamate into a single strong waterproof joint. Various materials are used to make these tapes, the more popular being polyisoibutelene (PIB), polythene and butyl rubber.

The first two will withstand really high voltages (up to 35,000 volts), while butyl rubber is designed for the low and medium voltages normally used by modellers. A range of thickness from 0.5 to 3mm and widths from 20 to 50mm will meet most needs.

Double-sided tape

Double-sided tape has adhesive on both sides of a thin carrier or foam, with a peel-off paper backing on both sides. Foam thickness is typically 0.8mm and this type of tape is available as strips or rolls. One with a flexible polypropylene base, only 0.1mm thick, is also useful.

Servo tape, used by radio control enthusiasts to mount their servos in models, has a much thicker foam layer, some 5mm thick, to help absorb the adverse effects of vibration.

Foam tape

Synthetic foam sealing tapes come in rolls with adhesive on one side and are designed to prevent the passage of dust, dirt and moisture. The foam may be PTFE based for higher temperature applications, polythene for general-purpose use or foam rubber for greater resilience.

Thread-sealing tape

Pure PTFE tape is now the first choice for sealing threaded joints and is widely used by plumbers. It is thin, conformal and works up to 260°C with most liquids and gases. It has the added advantage of reducing corrosion between dissimilar metals when threaded together.

Packing tape

PVC and polypropylene tapes, some of the latter reinforced with monofilament glass fibre, with rubber- or acrylic-based adhesives are designed for closing and sealing cartons and bags, but also have many other applications in modelling.

Velcro tape

Velcro is familiar as pairs of strips, one of small plastic hooks and the other similar loops. Pressing the strips together causes the hooks to engage the eyes, holding the pieces together. It is easy to part the strips with a peeling action.

Rolls of separate Velcro hook and loop components, usually 20mm wide with self-adhesive or heat-sensitive adhesive and a peel-off paper backing, have many applications where touch and close is the key requirement. There is also a form suitable for sewing in place on fabrics.

Chapter 5 Heat forming and vacuum forming

Using heat

You can shape, bend and form any thermoplastic to make customised parts by applying heat. It is possible, but not recommended, to work suitable materials just by heating them with a naked flame from a small butane torch. You will, however, need to take care of the noxious fumes they give off, not to mention the risk of them catching fire. Good ventilation and adequate facilities for extinguishing any fire are essential.

Although specialist heating equipment is not essential, a custom-built heater is often more socially acceptable than the domestic cooker and both are certainly safer than a naked flame. The most important requirement is that you can select the temperature.

Domestic ovens are thermostatically controlled and often have a built-in fan to ensure an even temperature. You can also make your own heater using an electric fire or stove element. Another possibility is to use a heat gun of which there are three categories:

- Hair dryers
- Heat-shrink guns
- Paint strippers

These three are listed in order of heat output and particular care is needed with a paint stripper to avoid melting the plastic.

The most widely used sheet materials for heat forming are ABS, butyrate and styrene, although others are now finding favour. The ideal temperature to work at is approximately 120°C – just over boiling point. Most plastics melt around at 200°C so take care not to apply too much heat in your haste to finish the job. It is better to use a lower temperature and do the work in stages. You can always reheat an item if it has not formed as expected.

For some low melting point plastics, you can even use a bowl of hot water as the heat source. You will need a suitable diameter former and a means of securing the sheet around the former while it is immersed in the water to produce a permanent bend.

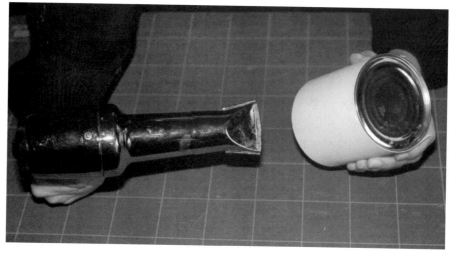

Figure 5.1 A heat-shrink gun which you can use to bend thermoplastics and tighten heat-shrink materials. You should wear protective gloves for this job.

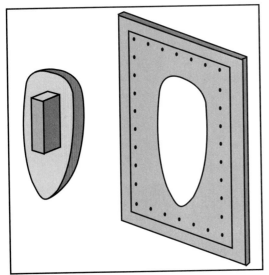

Figure 5.2 A wooden form and template for heat moulding.

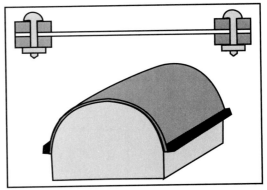

Figure 5.3 Clamping a sheet of plastic between strips of wood (top) and pulling it over a curved form (bottom) will allow you to make the curve permanent with the heat from a hot-air gun.

It is not always necessary to use heat to form a curve in plastics. You can bend most of them even when they are cold, although you will leave a degree of stress remaining in the curved material. You need to know when the plastic has reached its bending limit. ABS and some other thermoplastics have an in-built limit indicator. They go white just before they snap.

Cooling

Hot plastics retain heat for quite a long time, so give them time to cool before handling them or removing them from their mould. Wear thick protective gloves to avoid the risk of a nasty burn.

'IF YOU WANT YOUR DINNER ...
...YOU'LL HAVE TO LET ME USE MY OVEN!'

Bending

To produce a cylindrical shape from flat sheet is also relatively easy. You can form a single curvature by pulling the heated plastic over a simple former or even by allowing the plastic to sag into a hollow form. It is important only to heat the area of the material which you intend to bend.

Heat sealing cord and thread

You can stop nylon or terylene chord and thread from untwisting by heating the end briefly in a naked flame, when the plastic will melt and form a blob on the end. Take care, however, as if you are overzealous, a blob of molten material can give you, the furniture or the floor a nasty burn.

Heat forming

Before you start, remember that you can cut many household and food containers to provide useful pre-formed components. A good example is the use of part of a one-litre lemonade bottle for a windscreen.

Sometimes, it is possible to find a plastic extrusion and modify its shape to meet your requirements. A typical example is an exhaust stub on a scale model racing car. Make a form by shaping a length of wood. Find a suitable piece of plastic, which may be round tube or a piece of cable conduit with an oval cross-section. Push the tube onto the form and warm with a heat gun until the plastic takes on the required shape. Cut to the size you require. The arrow in Figure 5.5 shows where this has been done.

For more complex forming, you will have to make a plug and a template through which the form will pass; larger by twice the thickness of the plastic you will use for the moulding. You can cut the template from a piece of plywood or hardboard and firmly attach the plastic sheet. Heat the plastic evenly until it just starts to sag, remove the heat and quickly force the plug through the template and leave to cool.

Clearly, you cannot form as deeply using heat alone as you can with vacuum forming, and you will need to push the plug through the template further than you might initially think necessary to allow you to remove the crinkled bottom edge

Figure 5.4 A small, commercially available heater which is ideal for jobs that are not too large.

of the moulding. As often as not just heating the material and pulling it over a form will suffice, providing the form is not too deep.

For heat or vacuum forming most parts, the key plastics include ABS, acrylic, acetate, butyrate, copolyester, polycarbonate, PVC and styrene in thin sheet form. Material 0.75, 1, 1.5 and 2mm (30, 40, 60 and 80 thou) thick are the most useful.

Vacuum forming

Vacuum forming is one of the best processes if you are an amateur modeller and want to make a

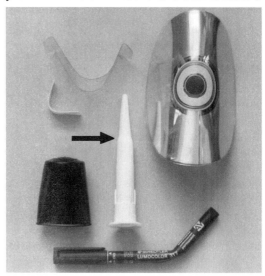

Figure 5.5 All these items have easily been reshaped with a heat gun.

Figure 5.6 *The front half-form for the WWII pilot shown in Figure 5.7. (Photo courtesy Vortex Plastics)*

Figure 5.7 *The complete vacuum-formed figure once the front and rear halves are glued together. (Photo courtesy Vortex Plastics)*

complex shape from a thermoplastic. You will need access to a vacuum-forming machine or, if you are that way inclined, you can fairly easily build your own.

Equipment

The actual forming of items requires the suction of a partial vacuum. Many schools now own vacuum-forming machines. They will usually allow their use if your child or a friend's child is at the school and you provide all the materials and sometimes a small contribution to school funds in cash or kind.

The alternative is to make your own machine. This is not as difficult as it sounds, since you can obtain the vacuum by temporarily connecting your household vacuum cleaner. Figure 5.8 shows a suitable design incorporating an electric heating element. If you have any doubt about your electrical skills, get a professional electrician to wire up the heater for you.

Forms

Plug design is important in terms of strength and avoiding reverse curves which make it impossible to remove the finished component from the form. Also, when forming the final item, there will be a thickness of plastic material between the plug and the outer surface of the moulding. This will inevitably result in some loss of detail.

To produce a finished item, you first have to produce a form of the item you wish to make. The common male form should be smaller than the final item by twice the thickness of the material you use to make it. A female form is uncommon and should be similarly larger.

Any blemish on the plug will show as an imperfection on the finished plastic item. While you can make the form from balsa wood, for example, it will require a tough glossy finish, which is easily obtained from a coating of epoxy resin, which is then sanded and polished to the required finish. Alternative materials include jelutong and pine.

Forming

Cut a piece of plastic suitably sized for the job with an adequate allowance (50mm) all round and mount it in the frame. Place it in the vacuum-forming machine above the mould and turn on the heater. When the plastic just starts to sag, turn on the vacuum which quickly forces the plastic down over the mould.

Speed is of the essence to avoid giving time for the plastic to cool before it is completely formed. Turn off the heater and vacuum pump and allow everything to cool before removing the finished item from the form. Finally cut off any waste material.

Figure 5.8
Top, a typical
h o m e - m a d e
vacuum-form-
ing machine
and, below
left, the way
the hot plastic
is pulled over
the form by the
vacuum.

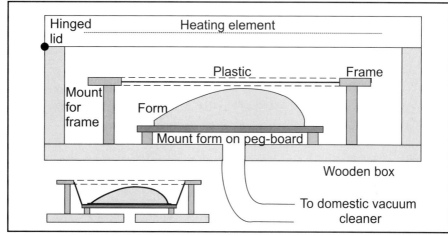

Casting

You can heat suitable plastics like ABS or styrene until they melt and then pour the molten liquid into a silicone rubber mould. It is a smelly business, the plastic is slow to heat up and melt and the results are only reasonable for simple shapes.

Heat joining

You can join thermoplastic belt or tubing using a hot knife blade between the ends, which you must cut square. This is ideal for making machinery drive belts and thin tyres for scale models of early vehicles and aircraft.

Hot glue

Hot glue is a thermoplastic form of adhesive. A hot-glue gun heats a stick of plastic glue until it is liquid, when you can pump it out of the gun to form a joint. There are a number of different glue stick plastics suited to joining a wide range of materials. More details are given in Chapter 4.

Heat-shrink covering materials

Many aeromodellers, and a few yacht modellers, use a heat-shrink film or fabric to cover part or all of their models. These materials are self-coloured, fuel proof, iron-on and usually self-adhesive.

Name	Type	Self adhesive	Wt gsm
Nylon	Nylon	No	30
Airspan	Polyester tissue (needs a light coat of dope)	No	24
Litespan	Tough synthetic material to replace tissue/dope	No	30
Fibafilm	Super-light, fibre-reinforced polyester film	No	42
Solarfilm	Iron-on plastic film with smooth glossy surface	Yes	55 - 70
Solarspan 2000	Multi-layer, heavy-duty iron-on film, 50% stronger than Solarfilm	Yes	65 - 75
Solartex	Iron-on fabric	Yes	85 - 95
Glosstex	Iron-on fabric with high gloss fuel-proof paint finish	Yes	120 - 130
Solarkote	Iron-on polyester film	Yes	70 - 80

***Table 5.1** The popular range of covering materials made by Solarfilm compared with nylon. Similar materials are produced by other companies under other names.*

Figure 5.9 Final tightening of Solartex heat-shrink fabric on a wing using a specialist iron.

Their weights and strengths vary considerably as Table 5.1 shows. Dark colours are lighter in weight than pale ones but heavier than transparent colours. Some iron-on materials have no adhesive backing, Paint around the surface you are covering with a heat-sensitive glue, such as Balsaloc, and iron on as usual.

You will need an iron, preferably like the one shown in Figure 5.9 and, ideally, a heat gun. A special thermometer will allow you to set your iron to the right temperature. Alternatively, use a scrap of covering material on the iron and increase the heat until it just starts to curl. Any serious overheating damages the tightening properties of the material and may melt it.

The final finish of any model reflects the surface finish below the covering, so make sure your preparatory work is thorough. Before starting, mentally divide the surface you will be covering into manageable sections. Make patterns from scrap paper before cutting out the covering material, allowing some 25mm for material overlaps.

Remove the transparent protective backing and place the film or fabric, adhesive side down, on the surface you are covering. Avoid creases or slackness while you use an iron to tack the edge of the covering in place. Iron down the edges,

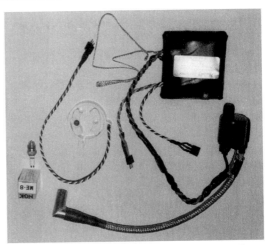

Figure 5.10 This electronic ignition system shows the use of heat-shrink tubing on both the leads and the battery pack. (Photo courtesy Just Engines)

trimming excess material with scissors or a craft knife and pulling it tight when smoothing around a curve.

With a heat-shrink gun, direct hot air to tighten the material, moving the gun rapidly about 100mm above the covering. Do not get the gun too close to the covering or stop moving it as you may melt a hole in the material. You can do this tightening job with a household or specialist iron but it is not as easy or quick. Aim for a taut finish with the edges carefully stuck down. Some materials shrink more strongly than others but all require you to pull the material nice and tight during the tacking process. Do not pull unevenly when tacking as this tends to produce warps.

When using shiny film materials, secure overlaps by first painting them with an etchant like Prymol and, when dry, ironing down the overlap.

Heat-shrink sleeving

A specialist application of heat-shrink materials is the tubing used to protect soldered joints in wires and to encase the battery packs used in electrically powered models and in radio control systems. This tubing is cut and positioned before the application of heat to the tubing shrinks it neatly, tightly and firmly in place.

Chapter 6 Rubber moulds and components

There are three types of material which are well suited to making self-releasing flexible moulds; silicone rubber, hot-melt vinyl and latex materials. Silicone rubber is the most expensive but also lasts longest and gives the best reproduction quality. All these materials need a form from which you can make your mould.

Silicone rubber

Cold-cure silicone rubber has many applications to modelling. Perhaps the most common use is to make flexible moulds for resin or low-melt metal casting. At the other extreme, you can use the material directly for the main access hatch seal on a model submarine hull.

It is the flexibility and resilience of silicone rubber that makes its application to model making so popular. With three exceptions, all the silicone rubber materials described below are those available from Alec Tiranti. The exceptions are silicone bath sealant which is a pre-mixed rubber that you can buy in DIY stores, silicone rubber O-rings which you will find in engineering supply, car accessory and some DIY shops, and flexible silicone tube available at model shops. These are described at the end of this chapter.

Storage, handling and mixing

If you keep your silicone rubber cool in closed tins it will store for half a year. You can improve this time to around a year by refrigeration. Keep the catalyst bottles airtight and avoid opening them for longer than necessary. Both ingredients are potentially dangerous. Do not swallow them, let them get into your eyes, breathe in their fumes or allow them regular contact with your skin. It is sensible to wear protective rubber gloves.

You should carefully measure the required quantities of silicone rubber and catalyst by volume before mixing them together. Calibrated beakers and spoons are available though some

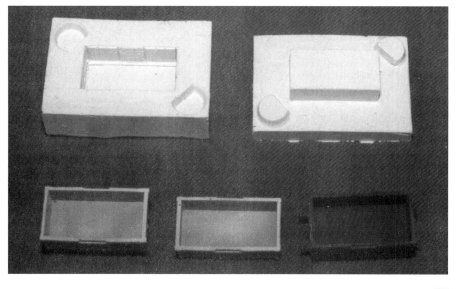

Figure 6.1 A small silicone rubber mould and a pair of small resin-cast railway wagon bodies produced from it.

catalysts are measured in drops. The manufacturer will provide detailed instructions about the correct ratios.

Always stir the rubber and the catalyst separately before thoroughly mixing them together. Try to avoid trapping in air during mixing. Some rubber/catalyst combinations are designed to become thixotropic, so make sure you mix them quickly before this thickening occurs.

Thickening, thinning and colouring

You can thin down silicone rubber with up to 10% silicone fluid (SF-96-50) which you mix with the rubber just before adding the catalyst. This will reduce the viscosity of the rubber and also increase both working and cure times. You can equally easily thicken silicone rubber and make it thixotropic by adding a maximum of 2% Tixo TA1. Experience will help you to judge whether thickening or thinning is necessary.

You can colour white silicone rubbers with Maestro acrylic/PVA polymers, which come in a very wide range of colours. You can even paint cured rubber with them, provided the rubber is perfectly clean. You can also add aniline black to simulate rubber tyres.

Release agents

You do not normally need a release agent with silicone rubber moulds. However, the inside of a mould box benefits from a release coating, such as the aerosol spray DP 100/2. You can make your own release agent by mixing 5% petroleum jelly (Vaseline) with white spirit in a small container stood in a bowl of hot water, stirring until the jelly dissolves.

When pouring silicone rubber onto itself, for example in a two-part mould, a release agent is essential. Allow the agent to dry before pouring rubber. Do not brush rubber over an area treated with release agent as you will disturb the protective wax layer.

When making the second half of a two-piece mould, brush rubber onto the pattern and allow it to trickle onto the surroundings. Silicone rubber also sticks to materials like plasticine, which you can varnish prior to coating it with release agent.

Making a mould

Although you can often purchase ready-made moulds, you will probably want to make your own. Assuming you have created your original, you can

' IT'S MY REPLACEMENT PARTNER !'

then produce a silicone rubber mould from it. The life of the mould you make depends on the type of silicone rubber you use, your choice of casting material and, in particular, the temperature of the casting material. A rubber like RTV 31 will last for many metal casts.

You can make your original pattern from almost any material but seal it first if it is porous. Make sure the surface of your pattern is perfectly clean, as it will reproduce any small imperfection; even a fingerprint.

Silicone rubber takes several days to develop its full properties so, although you can use the mould once it has cured, for producing large numbers of casts you should wait until it has fully cured.

Single-piece moulds

The simplest moulds are single-piece ones. Use RTV-11 unless you want a deep undercut or expect to use the mould a lot, in which case RTV-420 is better. Place your pattern in a box made from wood, sheet metal or Lego bricks securely pressed together and fixed to a base with double-sided tape.

Ensuring that the mould is level, slowly pour catalysed silicone rubber into a corner of the box, allowing the rubber to flow around the pattern. To minimise air bubbles if you have a deep undercut or intricate detail, brush a layer of rubber onto the pattern just before you pour the rest. When

the pattern is half covered wait a few minutes for the rubber to level. Continue pouring until you have covered the top of the pattern with some 6mm of rubber and leave to cure.

Two-piece moulds

You will need to make a two-piece mould for a figure of a human or animal. Half embed the figure in modelling wax or clay inside a mould box, leaving some 12mm clearance all round and remembering to include small conical alignment points for later mould assembly. With the mould level, pour in catalysed rubber until about 12 mm above the highest point of the pattern and leave to cure.

Without removing the pattern, invert the mould box and remove the wax or clay. Treat the exposed silicone rubber with release agent and refill the box with a fresh mix of rubber. Once the mould has cured, remove it from the box, part the two halves and remove the pattern.

A funnel-shaped reservoir at the top of a mould helps force the casting material into the detail. You must cut vents with a sharp knife or special gouge-shaped sprue cutter to allow trapped air to escape and help the free flow of the material inside the mould. A trial casting will show if

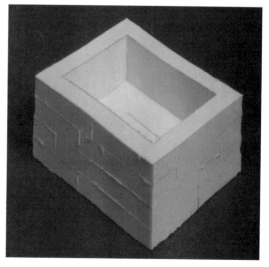

Figure 6.2 *The original item in a mould box made from Lego. The front is removed for clarity. (Photo courtesy Alec Tiranti Ltd.)*

Figure 6.3 *The completed mould ready to go back in its Lego box for immediate use. (Photo courtesy Alec Tiranti Ltd.)*

the mould has filled or whether you need to cut further vents or enlarge your existing ones.

Strip-off skin moulds

Skin moulds use a rather different approach and are ideal if you are working with a complex figure or need to produce a large mould. You can use RTV-428 to make strip-off skin moulds or the rather stronger RTV-420 if your original is deeply undercut, made thixotropic by mixing with Tixo TA1.

For a simple open mould, mount the pattern on a flat board and paint catalysed rubber all over the pattern, with plenty at the bottom edge of the mould. When cured, paint on another good layer. You can reinforce the whole mould or just parts of it with fabric, ensuring the rubber squeezes through the fabric mesh. When cured, you should make a plaster case, which you may also reinforce with fabric.

For figures such as a cavalryman's horse, farm, circus or fairground animals, you will need a two-part mould and a two-piece mould case. You should make a fence in modelling wax or clay round the centre line of the animal, complete with indentations for mould alignment. Brush on catalysed rubber, building up layers until you have a good thickness.

Once the rubber has cured, make a further row of indentations in the fence to align the mould case. A GRP case will not stick to silicone rubber. Use a layer of gel coat and two of chopped strand mat over both the rubber and the fence.

Once the GRP has cured, remove the fence and, after adding release agent to the mating surface of the mould and case, repeat the process for the second half. Finally, remove the rubber skin mould from the outer case and carefully slit down the inside of each leg to enable you to remove the finally cast animal. You should wet the finished mould with soapy water before pulling the rubber off inside-out.

There is more information about working with GRP in the next chapter as well as casting with resin.

Items from silicone rubber

It is in its ability to form a wide range of seals that silicone rubber is also widely used. From oil

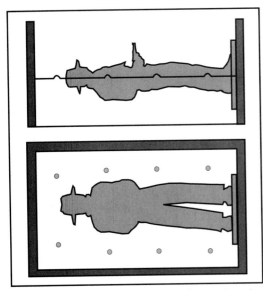

Figure 6.4 Side and plan views of a cowboy figure half-buried in clay, showing the locating cones. The figure's base is placed flush with the side of the mould box to avoid having to cut a pour hole in the finished mould.

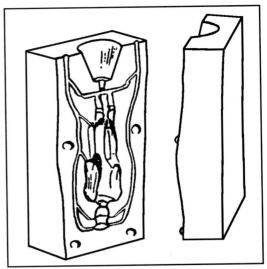

Figure 6.5 A typical example of a mould for a figure with a reservoir and air vents cut, ready for casting in low-melt metal. (Picture courtesy Alec Tiranti Ltd.)

seals on removable engine and gearbox covers to submarine hatch seals, silicone rubber is an ideal material. You will either have to build a mould in situ and treat it with release agent or, if the seal is circular, turn up a form in wax on a lathe. However, many different sizes of O-rings are readily available as is a wide range of seals.

Silicone rubber tube is popular for feeding fuel to glow plug engines as it is not attacked by the fuel. As it is relatively impervious to heat, it is also suitable for water, oil and even steam pipes.

Figure 6.7 Part of a silicone rubber submarine hatch seal which has been cast in situ.

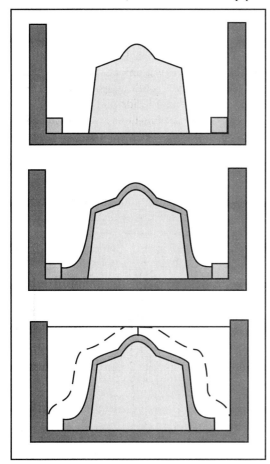

Figure 6.6 The three stages of making a strip-off skin mould. First, fix the form into a mould box with 12mm packing around the inside of the base of the box. Next, paint on two coats of silicone rubber. Finally, either fill the mould with plaster or put on reinforced plaster to the dotted line.

Figure 6.8 With a figure like a horse, start by making a fence around its centre line. Paint silicone rubber over the horse until sufficiently thick and then make a GRP case. Remove the fence and repeat for the second side.

Figure 6.9 Arrows point to silicone rubber tube used for the fuel feed and to connect the silencer to the flexible metal exhaust pipe.

Encapsulation

Silicone rubber has regularly been used to stop electronic components suffering from vibration on printed circuit boards. Placed liberally over exposed components, it will hold them securely in place. Though not aesthetically attractive, it is a much simpler proposition than full encapsula-

Figure 6.10 A thermostatically-controlled pot for hot-melt vinyl. (Photo courtesy Alec Tiranti Ltd.)

tion and does not have as much effect on heat dissipation. A typical example of this is shown in Figure 16.6 on page 140.

Hot-melt vinyl

Hot-melt vinyl is a re-usable synthetic rubber available in a variety of flexibilities; the more flexible materials are generally less durable. You can easily clean, cut up and re-melt redundant old moulds for re-use.

The main limitation of hot-melt vinyls is that your original must be able to withstand temperatures around 130°C to 180°C, depending on the grade you select. Molten rubber can cause severe burns, so always wear thick protective gloves and work in a well-ventilated room.

You will not usually need a release agent but you should seal porous forms with heat-resistant varnish. Damp clay is ideal for making patterns. but if you use plaster, you should soak your form in water and then dry it to prevent the vinyl sticking. Make a retaining box around your form from melamine-coated chipboard, sealing the joints with damp clay. When you pour the vinyl, keep some extra clay handy to seal any leaks, using a knife to avoid burning yourself.

Melt the vinyl in a double-skinned pot. Hot air between the skins melts the vinyl in the inner section. Cut the solid vinyl into small pieces before melting and heat slowly. Stir frequently, covering the container between stirring. A kilo of vinyl takes around half-an-hour to melt, producing a thin, creamy liquid. Avoid overheating and decomposing the vinyl, which results in dark streaks in the liquid and acidic fumes. Severe overheating will ignite the vinyl.

Pour the hot liquid around the form rather than directly onto it to avoid trapping air bubbles. Cover the form to a depth of around 30mm. Warming the pattern before pouring reduces the risk of voids in the mould. After the mould has cooled over night it is ready for use.

Latex

Latex is natural liquid rubber which dries when exposed to air. It is ideal for making thin, flexible

Figure 6.11 A fine model of a horse cast in a hot-melt vinyl mould. (Photo courtesy Alec Tiranti)

moulds by dipping the form into liquid latex. As only a thin film will cling to your form, you should carry out successive dipping until you reach the thickness you need.

Allow the latex to dry naturally for twenty-four hours before removing it from the form, since it loses its elasticity if overheated. The mould will peel off the form more easily if rinsed in soapy water. Allow to dry before use.

You can make patterns of polyester resin, clay or plaster. Do not use metal for the form as it spoils the properties of the latex. If you use a plaster form, you can make a mould in one dip by leaving the pattern suspended in the latex. It will take about half an hour for a 150mm high figure.

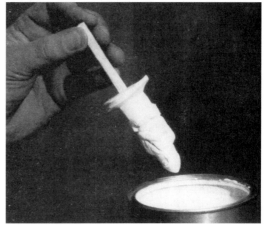

Figure 6.12 You can dip a figure into latex to make a skin mould. (Photo courtesy Scott Bader)

Chapter 7 Composite materials and resin casting

Glass reinforced plastic

GRP or, as it is often called, fibreglass is a useful material in most areas of modelling. GRP has always been popular in working models, such as boat hulls, car and diesel locomotive bodies and various aircraft parts, such as cowls and wheel spats. Even some complete airframes are made from it. You can also use it to add strength in these models around internal combustion engine bays and other stressed areas. GRP is particularly useful if you need a number of identical copies of an original item.

You can also use GRP and its resins for many other applications such as casting and repairing a wide range of materials including GRP itself. It is ideal for making items like a PCB etching bath or a coolant tray for a lathe or milling machine. Flat laminate is widely used for making electronic printed circuit boards and equally useful for making small items like control horns for models operated by radio.

GRP is a composite material made by placing glass fibres, in the form of matting or fabric, into a mould and bonding the fibres together with resin. While it takes a fair amount of effort to make a plug and mould, subsequent production of multiple units is not a lengthy task; a benefit if you need more than one part or plan to build more than one similar model.

There are two different types of resin, polyester and epoxy, and both of these come in the form of gel-coat and laying-up resin. There are also more specialist clear-casting resins. Epoxy resins are generally harder to use than polyester ones but

`No, it's not an alien.... it's my husband prepared to do some fibreglassing!'

provide better strength and impact resistance, particularly when used with a suitable filler.

The strength of any finished item depends on the quantity and type of resin you use, as well as the amount and type of the glass reinforcement, which is generally in one of three forms:

1. Chopped strand mat – random direction, non-woven glass fibres, typically 50mm long. This category includes tissue.
2. Plain weave fabric – fibres woven in two directions at right angles. This includes ribbon as well as cloth.
3. Rovings – fibres all running in a single direction.

Several properties make GRP an attractive material for use in a range of modelling applications.

- Suitable for complete structures as well as small components.
- High strength and resilience combined with low weight.
- Dimensionally stable.
- Resists most chemicals including fuels, oils and weather.
- Self-colouring or metallised finish easily achieved.
- Easy to make without costly equipment.
- Ideal for making several identical items.
- Able to pass radio signals.

Figure 7.1 A typical GRP hull clearly showing the pattern of the planks.

Designing the moulding and mould

In making any model or part of a model from GRP, you should consider just how much strength you require and the weight you can accept. You should also think about how you are going to produce a practical mould. The strength and weight will, of course, both have a direct influence on the thickness of the resulting finished component.

It is essential to have a degree of taper on any form. This should be a minimum of around 5° if you are planning to use a single-piece mould. You will have to use a two-piece mould if there is any serious undercut. This is shown in Figures 7.2 and 7.3.

Figure 7.2 You must build some degree of taper into any mould for GRP or use a two-part mould.

Figure 7.3 The ship hull, left, is readily released from a one-piece mould, whereas that on the right requires a two-piece mould.

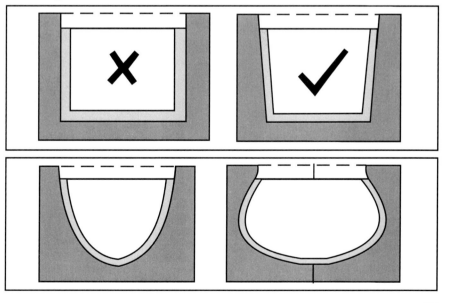

Figure 7.4 An unusual shape of GRP engine cowl for a radio controlled model aircraft.

Designing in strength

Sometimes you may want a GRP moulding that is relatively thin for weight reasons, but with adequate stiffness and rigidity. Examples include a racing hull for a yacht or speed boat, or the fuselage of a radio controlled jet aircraft. You can incorporate these features in the form of the moulding itself. Semi-circular, oval and curved cross-sections are inherently longitudinally stiff. You should, however, avoid sharp corners as it is hard to get the GRP to fill these and they are vulnerable to damage.

You can increase stiffness locally by building up extra layers of reinforcement in the areas where you want more strength. You should increase the cross-section progressively to give a gradual change of shape. An abrupt build-up introduces weakness at the point of change of section. You should not attempt to join GRP mouldings edge-to-edge but use an overlap design instead. These features are shown in Figure 7.5.

Moulding thickness

When working with chopped strand mat, you can pre-calculate the thickness of a moulding quite accurately. Estimating the thickness of other forms of laminate is harder, particularly for mixtures of cloth, mat or rovings. Table 7.1 provides some data for varying weights of mat and gives some guidance for other materials.

Weight

The weight of a particular part may or may not be of consequence. Certainly it is important in any component for a flying model aircraft and also for many classes of boat, particularly out-and-out speed models and racing yachts. For a submarine hull, it tends to be unimportant, as most boats require ballast to remain under water. You can calculate weight from Table 7.2, knowing the surface area of the mould and the number of layers in the finished laminate.

Strength

The strength and directional properties of a GRP laminate depend on the type of reinforcement you use, the resin-to-glass ratio and the resin type. It

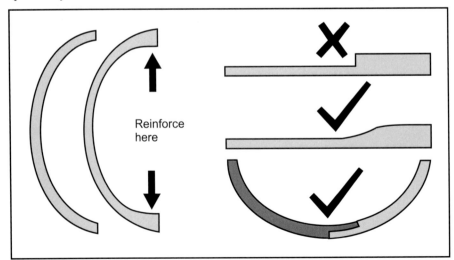

Reinforce here

Figure 7.5 A curved shape gives natural lengthways strength. You can increase this strength with edge reinforcement. Right, make sure reinforcement is gradual and use overlapping joints.

Layers	gsm	mm	gsm	mm
1	127	0.4	300	0.6
2		0.75		1.2
3		1		1.8
1	200	0.4	450	1.0
2		0.8		2.0
3		1.2		3.0

Table 7.1 The thickness of any chopped strand mat laminate depends on the weight and number of layers of mat as well as using a reasonable amount of resin.

Material	gsm	Weight in gsm of 1 layer + gel coat
Chopped strand mat	300	1626
	450	2166
Plain weave fabric	127	1006
	200	1191
	300	1347
Woven rovings	290	1337
	600	1870

Table 7.2 The weights of various different types of GRP laminate.

also depends on how you actually carry out the work. Reinforcing materials divide into three main groups:

Unidirectional – The fibres of rovings lie in a single direction to give maximum strength.

Bi-directional – In woven and ribbon fabrics, the strands are interlaced in two different directions. These fabrics are less strong than unidirectional fibres and the strength is often greater in one direction than in the other.

Random – The fibres of chopped strand mat and of tissue are oriented haphazardly, providing the weakest laminate. It is, however, the easiest to use when making any sort of complex moulding.

Resins

Polyester resin

Polyester resin is easy and economic to use, but does produce a very strong and distinctive smell which many people dislike and is also highly inflammable. It will only cure at temperatures above 15°C. You should use the same resin for fixing items like formers to GRP made with this resin. You can, however, fix attachments with epoxy resin provided the original GRP item has cured for at least a fortnight.

Epoxy resin

Epoxy resin is relatively odour free and is used for stronger and more impact-resistant GRP construction as well as items made from carbon fibre and kevlar. You should always use this same resin for attaching fixtures. Epoxy resin is rather harder to work successfully into the glass material than polyester resin.

Acrylic resin

These relatively new resins are just starting to compete with polyester as laminating resins. Their big advantage is their lower shrinkage rate.

Figure 7.6 This viscous-looking working shark is made largely from GRP and is indicative of the range of uses of this material.

67

Additives

A number of additives are useful for altering the characteristics of the resin used to make composite materials. Avoid inhaling dust when sanding the hardened mix with or without any of these additives.

Colloidal silica

This fine lightweight (0.05g/cc) white powder is added to resin to make it thixotropic. Its uses include making fillets and fairings. A mixing ratio of around 1 part colloidal silica to 2 parts mixed resin suits most purposes. The resulting mixture can benefit from the addition of up to 4 parts micro-balloons.

Micro-fibres

Cellulose fibres, weighing around 0.15g/cc, when added to resin in the ratio 3 part mixed resin to 1 part micro-fibres, make an ideal low-viscosity adhesive for attaching ply formers to GRP.

Micro-balloons

Small lightweight (0.25g/cc) hollow glass or phenolic spheres may be added to the resin making it suitable for use as a lightweight filler or for making fairings and fillets.

Metal and stone powders

You can simulate a metallic finish with GRP by mixing the appropriate powdered metal into the resin before adding the catalyst. In the same way you can obtain finishes which simulate marble, onyx and slate.

Carbon fibre and kevlar

The strength of GRP comes from its embedded strands of glass, but even tougher composites are feasible using carbon fibres or kevlar instead. With this greater strength also comes an increase in cost and the need to use epoxy rather than polyester resin.

Kevlar is an immensely strong, lightweight fibre and is widely used to make body armour. Carbon fibres were developed for the aerospace industry and are a pure form of carbon having a diameter of less than 10 microns. Carbon fibres are available in the form of cloth, tape or tows of unidirectional fibres. Carbon fibre rod is also available commercially in the form of archery arrows and fishing rod lengths which may suit some modelling applications. You can even get hybrid weaves made from a mixture of kevlar and carbon fibre.

Figure 7.3 compares strength-to-weight ratio, using the same amount of resin, of these two materials and GRP made from chopped strand mat. Kevlar and carbon fibre are clearly stronger than GRP. However, the high price of these two materials means that you should use them sparingly to provide the greatest possible strength in highly stressed areas. A typical example is the reinforcement of the wings of a model glider, where you can glue carbon fibre tows in place to strengthen the main spar.

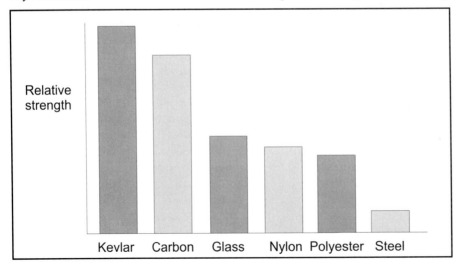

Table 7.3 A comparison of the strength to weight ratios of composite materials with some other plastics and steel.

Making the mould

The first stage in any fibreglass construction is to make yourself a mould. This normally requires a male plug from which you can then make a female mould. The final item is laid up in the female mould, so prepare yourself for a fair amount of work. You can make the plug from plaster of Paris, balsa wood, jelutong wood, expanded polystyrene or even clay.

To give a hard surface, you can cover the plug with a layer of epoxy resin. Any mark on the surface of the mould, no matter how small, will replicate itself on the piece of laminate you are forming over the mould. Time and patience spent getting a top-class finish to the surface will reward you well, though it may seem an awful lot of work if you only require a single component. Perhaps this is why the use of moulds is so popular for producing items in quantity. Because it is the part of the finished GRP item in contact with the moulding which needs a fine finish, once you have made a male plug, you should then produce a female mould from GRP and repeat the process of making the finished GRP item in this mould.

You will need to treat both the original plug and the female mould with a release agent. Up to six coats of wax, well polished in, followed by a coat of blue-coloured PVA release agent is the recommended route. You can also make moulds from self-releasing flexible materials like silicone rubber.

Fabrication methods

Working with composites can be unpleasant or even dangerous unless you take adequate safety precautions. Glass fibre particles irritate the skin as well as eyes and lungs. Polyester resins are both inflammable and poisonous. You should wear clothing that will protect your arms and neck as well as rubber gloves and safety goggles. If you have to sand GRP, a suitable dust mask is essential. Do not smoke when working with GRP and keep well clear of naked flames including pilot lights for boilers and heaters. Make sure you have a fire extinguisher handy and always work in a well-ventilated area.

Figure 7.7 Stippling-in resin on top of chopped strand mat to make a model boat hull. (Photo courtesy Scott Bader)

You will need an air temperature of at least 15°C to make GRP. It is either an outdoor summer job or one which you will have to do indoors. You must cut the glass fibre material to suit the mould, using several pieces for more complex shapes.

Coat the plug with gel-coat to give a fine finish and when it is tacky, add a coat of resin. Then place chopped strand mat, followed by further resin, using a stippling action to eliminate bubbles. When this is tacky, add another layer of glass and resin; sufficient for all but the largest moulds. Now patience becomes essential. Depending on the temperature, the resin sets in about an hour, but you should really wait a week before removing the mould from the plug. It seems an impossibly long time to wait, but don't risk ruining it.

You must also take great care how you release the completed mould to avoid scratching it. Always gently ease the edge of the mould from the plug with wooden or plastic wedges or even a plastic spatula. Introducing water between the mould and the original plug may help with the release process.

Finally clean and polish the mould, repairing any small imperfection with a filler like Isopon. Then treat the mould with wax and PVA release agent in the same way as the original plug.

Figure 7.8 Carefully removing a finished hull from the mould. (Photo courtesy Scott Bader)

The moulding

This is similar to making the mould but with the laminate inside the mould. Start with gel-coat and then add two layers of chopped strand mat; adequate unless you want an exceptionally strong final moulding. If you want a coloured finish, mix in the pigment before adding the catalyst. If the weight of the finished item is critical, be careful

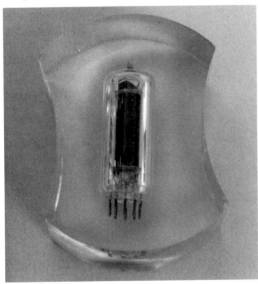

Figure 7.9 A thermionic valve from an early television set encapsulated in clear polyester resin.

not to use too much resin as this is where the weight lies. Remember, you can add partial additional layers to provide local reinforcement at potential stress points.

When you apply the gel-coat make sure you cover all internal corners and remove all air bubbles. Bubbles in the gel-coat leave a very thin surface skin which will either break immediately, leaving an indent or result in an air bubble just below the surface which will usually burst when the temperature rises. Remove the moulding after waiting the full week, using the same techniques as you used to release the mould from the plug, taking care not to damage either the mould or the moulding. You can then trim the final moulding.

Repairs

Polyester resin will bond to most material including ferrous and non-ferrous metals, wood and polyester-based GRP laminates and is therefore useful for repairing damaged models. The repair uses the same laminating technique involved when making a moulding.

For good adhesion, clean any oil and grease off the surface before starting work. For non-ferrous materials score the surface to provide a key and with ferrous materials you should also degrease them with acetone. Polyester resin will not stick to polythene, which you can use to advantage when making minor repairs.

Resin casting

Casting parts or models is usually done with a special polyester casting resin, which can be clear if you want a transparent item. Casting resin comes in two parts, the resin and the hardener which you must carefully mix in the correct proportions. You can also cast finely detailed items with lay-up resin and a suitable mould. You can thicken the resin by mixing in a standard or metallic filler, and colour it by adding a pigment. You can add up to 5g of pigment per 100g resin/filler mixture to colour it. You can even get casting resin to simulate a wood finish.

You can buy ready-made moulds for casting, or create your own from home-made forms. You

Figure 7.10 A clear resin coach, once painted, allows you to see through the windows . (Photo courtesy Cedric Verdon)

can make moulds from a variety of self-releasing flexible materials, where additional release agents are not necessary. As explained in the previous chapter, silicone rubber is ideal for this purpose.

You can bulk up and thicken resin by mixing it with a filler. This helps to reduce the temperature of the curing process. Apart from a standard filler powder, you can produce interesting effects with copper, aluminium, or brass powder which give a convincing metallic effect, while graphite will produce a weathered look.

If using standard filler, slowly add an equal quantity of filler to the resin. Keep stirring as you add the filler and when you have a consistent mix leave it for a few minutes to get rid of any air bubbles. Add the catalyst, stir the mixture and again allow it to stand before pouring it into the mould.

It is possible to trap air in parts of more complex moulds. You can minimise this by squeezing a flexible mould, starting at the bottom and working to the top. Take care with areas such as the tips of hands and ends of rifles. You can reinforce these with wire. If you make a large casting you should cast it in a number of layers to reduce the chances of shrinkage or distortion.

The mixture normally takes less than an hour to cure in a warm room. When set, peel the mould off to reveal the item moulded in resin. Then clean the mould; if it is of latex, wash it in soapy water and give the inside a light coat of talcum powder once it is dry.

Clear casting

You can use clear-casting resin to embed objects in transparent plastic, anything from electronic components to model figures, to protect these items for permanent display. You can also cast a range of vehicle bodies where you wish to see through the windows. You can add dyes in a wide range of colours to clear-casting resin.

Any item you are embedding must be clean, dry and free from oil or grease. When encapsulating biological specimens, you can dip insects in acetone, while you should dry plants and then seal them with polyurethane varnish. You should also varnish any paper items.

You will need a suitable mould. You can use a suitable household container or buy as a ready made item. You can purchase many different shapes of plastic mould including square, oblong, round, semi-circular and dome shaped. Do not use flexible rubber moulds which allow air to inhibit the resin, resulting in a tacky surface. You can use polythene containers but avoid polystyrene which the resin dissolves.

Catalyse some resin and pour into the mould to form a base layer. When this is a firm consistency, place any item you wish to encapsulate on it and pour a little more resin around it. A light specimen may float and need gluing to the base layer with a few drops of resin. In a very small casting, you can cover the item in a single pouring.

For larger ones build the casting up in a series of layers as a large amount of resin generates a lot of heat which may crack the casting. When the final layer is firm, cover it with polyester film or cellophane to exclude air and avoid a tacky surface. Leave to harden before removing the casting from the mould.

Figure 7.11 These resin-cast models of ships' figureheads use similar techniques to those needed to make an ornamental chess set.

Epoxy castings

Many people make small castings from epoxy glue in a silicone rubber mould. The use of a 24-hour adhesive rather than the rapid variety will produce the strongest casting, while the application of a little heat will help the epoxy flow into the detail. You can also make castings from the same epoxy resin used for making GRP.

Polyurethane resin castings

An alternative is to use polyurethane resin which results in a strong, durable casting with excellent definition and reproduction of fine detail. It is particularly useful for casting small-scale models due to its very low rate of shrinkage.

It costs more than polyester resin but is fast setting and easy to measure and mix. Its main advantage is that it is odourless, unlike polyester resin.

The main differences when using polyurethane rather than polyester resin are:

• Polyurethane sticks to self-releasing mould materials. Spray moulds with special release agent.
• Uncured resin is affected by moisture. Ensure moulds, mixing containers and tools are completely dry.
• Only use special non-absorbent fillers.
• The addition of pigments is not recommended. You can paint castings after they have cured.

The resin comes as a two-part kit, the resin base and the special catalyst. Measure equal amounts by weight or by volume into separate mixing cups and stir well. Mix the two parts, again thoroughly stirring. Pour into the mould immediately, as the mixture gels within 2-3 minutes, and leave to cure.

You can remove the casting from the mould in half-an-hour but allow it to cure for another 2 hours at room temperature.

You can file, polish, sand, and paint epoxy, polyester and polyurethane castings. If painting, thoroughly wash the polyurethane casting to remove traces of release agent. You can paint it with modelling enamels or acrylics.

Coatings

Epoxy resin is increasingly popular as a method of providing a fine and durable finish on a model constructed from wood. Two examples are the coating of a model boat hull or a wood-veneered model aircraft wing.

Particularly for a flying aircraft, where weight is critical, it is essential not to use too much resin because of the weight it adds to the structure. The use of an old credit card is ideal for smoothing a thin layer in place.

Once the resin has set, you can sand it with progressively finer wet and dry paper prior to polishing.

Chapter 8 Expanded polystyrene and other foams

Rigid foam

By far the most popular rigid foam used for modelling is expanded polystyrene. This is the white material, widely employed for packing consumer durables. It is used by modellers to build anything from hills on scenic layouts to light-weight flying models.

Blue, pink and green varieties of expanded polystyrene are denser, firmer and stronger foams, roughly twice the weight of the white variety and rather more expensive. They are also more resistant to knocks and dents. They are best for making highly stressed components like high aspect ratio aircraft wings. You should use them sparingly for applications where strength as well as weight are critical factors, though sometimes

you can reduce weight by hollowing out items. For most other purposes, the ordinary white foam is totally satisfactory.

You must protect expanded polystyrene with some form of skin as otherwise it is fragile and brittle. It is also easily dissolved by many adhesives, solvents and paints, so take care to ensure that what you use is compatible with expanded polystyrene. If in doubt, carry out a test on a small offcut.

To make a skin for a model landscape, a skimming of papier mâché is inexpensive. You can quickly build up hills from layers of foam glued on top of each other and then sand them to shape. For model aircraft, you can use heat-shrink film as a covering provided there are wooden leading

'JUST WHAT I NEED FOR MY NEW LAYOUT!'

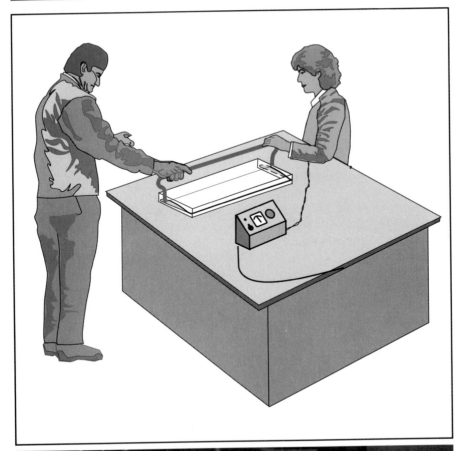

Figure 8.1 It is best for two people to work together to cut a wing core with a hot-wire cutter.

Figure 8.2 A professional computer-controlled foam wing cutter at work.

and trailing edge spars to take the flight loads. This can result in a lightweight solution which is useful for electric models. You can always cut additional lightening holes out of the foam. However, most wings are covered with a veneer of balsa or obeche.

You can make not only wings, fins, tailplanes but even complete flying models from the material. You can cover foam cores with heat-shrink film, brown paper, card, sheet balsa or obechi veneer. Most coverings are applied with a latex contact adhesive, such as Copydex, but do check to make sure that the glue does not dissolve the foam.

Cutting

There are several ways you can cut expanded polystyrene foam. For small items, a serrated knife such as a bread knife, worked with a sawing action will produce a relatively clean cut. You can also, with care, sand the material to shape. You can hollow out expanded polystyrene with a soldering iron.

For larger components, especially where accuracy is important, a hot-wire cutter is the only real solution. The hot-wire cutter may take the form of a hand-held bow or fixed cutter. Both use nichrome wire as the cutter, which is run at black heat from a low-voltage power supply. You can obtain a bow cutter and power supply from model shops which sell radio controlled model aircraft, or make your own bow and use a car battery charger to power it. You will need one or more templates to guide the hot wire.

Foam aircraft wings are fairly complex items to cut and give a clear understanding of how you undertake the task of cutting expanded polystyrene with a hot-wire bow. The end product is a wing which resists warping and can easily reproduce any chosen aerofoil section. All you need are templates for the root and tip ribs, your hot-wire bow and power supply. You will also want a clear flat working surface.

Start by roughly cutting a piece of foam a bit larger than the size you need for your wing. Next, prepare ply rib profiles with a short lead in at each end and pin them to the foam. You should anchor the foam block firmly in place with weights.

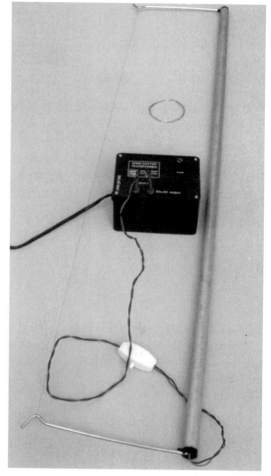

Figure 8.3 *A foam wing cutter and power supply suitable for home use.*

You will need a helper to assist you in feeding the hot wire through the foam. Start just above the top of the trailing edge of the rib at each end. With a slow continuous movement, move the wire right through the foam block.

At all times keep the wire pressed against the rib template. Try to maintain a constant speed of movement since the wire cuts by melting the foam. Too fast will cause dragging of the centre of the wire; too slow will result in a rough surface to the cut.

Turn the block over, using foam you have just removed to support the top profile of the wing core. Repeat the cutting process on the bottom of

Figure 8.4 A veneered foam wing with a cut-out for the undercarriage mount.

the block starting from the leading edge. You can then make any necessary cut-outs with a craft knife or by melting the foam with the tip of a soldering iron.

When skinning the cores, first lightly sand them and remove any dust. Having applied latex glue to the wing surface and skin panel, place a sheet of transparent polythene on top of the wing's glued surface to allow you to position the veneer before sliding out the polythene and permanently fixing the skin in place.

You can use a similar technique for cutting out any item from expanded polystyrene where the component size is important and where you do not need three-dimensional curves. You will find more information on this subject in David Thomas' comprehensive book ***Radio Control Foam Modelling*** (see Bibliography page 142).

The Maxicraft Hot Wire Cutter is a different type of device to a hot-wire wing-cutting bow. It looks like a power fret saw and you can use it in a very similar way. The cutter has a flat table on top of the main body, housing a transformer and the controls. The thin nichrome cutting wire feeds from a storage reel below the table to the top of a tubular 'U' shaped arm You can move the top connection allowing you to tension and adjust the length of the wire. The maximum thickness of foam you can cut is 200mm, with a throat of some

Figure 8.5 The Maxicraft Hot Wire Cutter, 4390 and some examples of the items you can cut with it. (Photo courtesy Minicraft Macford Products Ltd.)

350mm. You can tilt the 'U' shaped suspension arm sideways to enable you to make angled cuts. The sides and front of the table are grooved to fit home-made cutting guides.

The wire is powered from the built-in low voltage transformer and provides an adjustable voltage to suit varying foam densities and lengths of wire. As with a bow cutter, set the wire to a hot, black heat. Use a test sample, before embarking on your project, to check the heat and find the correct feed rate, which will be relatively slow. Too high a feed speed will bow the wire, reducing accuracy and spoiling the finish of the cut.

With practice, you can cut out shapes from flat sheet and produce more complex three-dimensional shapes. You can use cardboard templates to improve accuracy, especially when producing more than one identical part.

Shaping

You can sand expanded polystyrene, though it is a messy job producing a mass of small granules which tend to stick to anything else around because they become electrically charged. You also need to take care not to gouge out large chunks. On the other hand, removal of the material is quick and you can easily produce an accurate shape by regularly checking with templates cut from cardboard.

Adhesives

The danger you must avoid, when gluing expanded polystyrene, is that of dissolving the polystyrene with the adhesive. This will occur with most petroleum-based glues, but latex and water-based ones work well.

It is worth noting that it is sometimes helpful to use a foam core as a form for making GRP. If you use polyester resin, coat it well with emulsion paint to stop the polyester dissolving the polystyrene, but if you use epoxy resin, you can put it straight on. When the GRP has set, you can then dissolve out the expanded polystyrene with a solvent like acetone, leaving just the GRP.

Polyurethane foam

Polyurethane foam is widely used to fill the cavities in building construction for insulation and

Figure 8.6 Top, three different grades of commercial foam rubber, middle, a block of expanded polystyrene foam, bottom, a length of the foam used to insulate water pipes in houses and finally, right, a DIY can which produces copious amounts of polyurethane foam.

gap filling but is also ideal for filling the buoyancy tanks in boats and making hilly terrain on baseboards for railway and military modelling. You can make it by mixing equal quantities of a two-part liquid.

After mixing, the liquid rapidly expands to some twenty-five times its original volume resulting in a closed-cell foam. It is rigid, light and relatively waterproof. It is often used to prevent model boats sinking after they become waterlogged by pouring the mixture into suitable cavities within the hull.

The foam bonds to most materials and you can use it as a filler between the inner and outer of any double-skinned model. As with many other plastics, it will emit toxic fumes if heated. Aerosol cans of foam avoid the need for any mixing and can produce as much as forty times the volume of the can. The foam is set sufficiently for you to cut and shape it after 45 minutes and is fully cured in around three hours, when you can sand and paint it.

Soft foams

As far as the modeller is concerned, there are two basic grades of soft foam; those which collapse to virtually nothing when squeezed and those which are relatively firm. The former have applications such as upholstering dolls' house furniture and filling seats and cushions in model caravans and pleasure boats. The firmer grade is ideal for protecting vulnerable parts of radio control systems when installed in models. A serrated knife or band saw will cut the foam but hot-wire cutting will ruin it.

Figure 8.7 A fairly solid foam protects the radio receiver and battery pack in this model aircraft.

Chapter 9 Plastic kits and styrene

Plastic kits

For many people, their first serious introduction to modelling is the assembly one of the ubiquitous Airfix, Revell or other manufacturers' plastic kits. By far the most popular are aircraft, with kits of ships, land vehicles, spacecraft, military and fantasy all a long way behind. More specialist kits of buildings and line-side accessories are aimed primarily at railway modellers.

Styrene is almost invariably the plastic used, usually in two different forms. The raw styrene material is found in transparent parts like cockpits, headlight lenses and windows. The remainder of the kit uses high-impact styrene which includes colouring, a rubber additive to stop the plastic shattering and make it more resilient and, usually, a lubricant. You must remove this last item, often silicon based, prior to painting.

The kit components come attached to frames of plastic which allow a number of parts to be moulded at the same time. The lengths of plastic which attach the parts to the frame are known as sprue. A few specialist kits are vacuum formed from ABS. The tyres on land vehicles are generally made from PVC which provides the look and give of rubber.

These plastic kits are an excellent introduction to modelling for the young and the simpler kits are straightforward to assemble. The more complex kits can result in museum quality models if you take care with their construction and painting.

Figure 9.2 Concentrating on assembling the model.

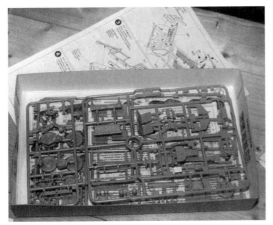

Figure 9.1 *The parts of this plastic kit, like the vast majority, are made from styrene.*

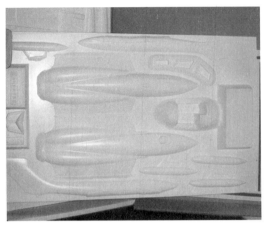

Figure 9.3 *A few kits, like this de Havilland Sea Vixen, are vacuum formed rather than injection moulded and produce excellent results.*

Do not under any circumstances try to paint a plastic kit with a cellulose-based paint or lacquer as it will craze the styrene and ruin the model – unless that happens to be the effect you are trying to achieve.

The most common size for aircraft kits is 1/72nd and you will find models of aeroplanes from the dawn of aviation to modern jet airliners with the majority covering First and Second World War combat aircraft. The models include aeroplanes made by all the industrialised nations but with the majority of American, British, German and Japanese types.

Car sizes vary from 1/32nd at the small end to 1/8th for the largest. However, the vast majority of cars are in the 1/12th or 1/25th scale. You can get kits of anything from a sports super-car to a Rolls-Royce, a Ford Model T or a drag racer. A typical car kit will include a single moulding for the main bodywork and several frames of associated parts. One of these frames will contain all the chromium or metallised parts and there will also be one for the transparent parts.

The tyres, as already mentioned, are almost invariably made from black PVC. There may even be the odd bits of metal for seat-belt parts and axles, complete with accompanying nylon bushes.

Finally, you will find some decorative decals. You may even find a material like nylon used to simulate the thin metal radiator grid. You can sometimes simulate vinyl roofs and upholstery using self-adhesive sheeting or even masking tape.

Ship models are made to a smaller scale as the originals can be up to 300 metres long. 1/144th is a popular scale resulting in a practical size for the majority of vessels. Ships from both the sail and steam era are widely available, with France, Spain and the UK the major powers in the sailing era while Germany, Japan, the USA, UK and the USSR, the major combatants in the two world wars, providing the majority of steam-powered warships.

Figure 9.4 *Models of spacecraft have increased in popularity since the 1960s.*

Figure 9.5 *Even small models of warships carry a great deal of detail.*

Assembly

Many inexperienced people start building plastic models by gluing them together with polystyrene cement and end up making a fine mess of the assembly of their first model. They also learn to recognise a fundamental problem with these kits; the need to clean off any flash or rough edges where the part has been cut from its frame. This former is more of a problem on kits with long production runs where the manufacturer's tooling has become worn. Fortunately, flash is easy to remove with a sharp modelling knife. There are two key factors in building from a kit. First, file, scrape, carve and cut the components until they fit together as well as possible. Second, don't use glue from a tube, apply a solvent with a fine paint brush.

Customised parts

Customising a kit and making additional parts, such as added interior detail, can both improve the final product and result in a unique model. Remember too that there are numerous specialist companies which produce a wide range of accessories in plastic that you can use if you are an avid modeller. By the very nature of the material used, it is not too difficult to make your own parts from the significant amounts of sprue left over from any kit. You can heat this with a heat gun or carefully over a naked flame and pull, bend, twist or push it into shape.

You can then file, sand or cut the component until it is exactly how you want it and glue it into place as if it were a component of the original kit. The alternative is to use styrene sheet, strip, rod or tube. These are widely available from model shops where they are found on special display stands like that shown in Figure 9.7. Finally you can use thin plastic-coated electrical wire to simulate items like ignition and fuel leads or brake and steam pipes on larger scale models.

The use of wet and dry emery paper is the best way to remove material from any part of a kit, such as a wing trailing edge which is too thick. Often, because of the moulding process, small parts like doors are far too thick for the correct scale. You can use the kit part as a template to cut a new part from thinner styrene sheet. You can also custom-build items like seats from thin

Figure 9.6 The builder of this World War II German tank has obtained plans and photographs of the original vehicle. The pieces come from two different kits, together with some scratch-built parts.

plastic. Pipes and electrical wiring are easily drawn out from sprue.

Chopping parts with a razor saw, removing a section and then rejoining the end parts is quite feasible, as is adding in a custom-made section to lengthen a part, using styrene sprue or sheet for making good the fit. Careful filing and sanding should make any joins invisible after painting.

Styrene materials

Because specialist styrene sheet, custom-made styrene building materials and detailed parts are widely available from model shops, it is worth

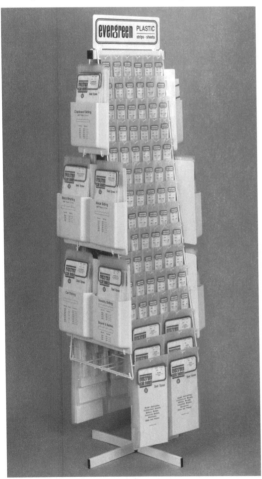

examining how to use this material for building models from scratch. The same techniques apply when modifying plastic kits and provide an excellent introduction to styrene modelling. Magazines such as **Scale Models International** and **Railway Modeller** carry articles on modifying boats, planes, armoured and other vehicles as well as buildings, locomotives, rolling stock and railway structures. You will find styrene is quicker and easier to use than other materials such as wood, card or metal.

You can purchase a wide range of styrene strips, sheets and a variety of extruded shapes made by companies like Evergreen, Plasticard and Plastruct. You can glue this opaque white styrene using the same solvents and cements you use for plastic kits, and paint them with the same types of paints. A variety of precision-cut strips and special sections is available for several of the common model scales. Details are given in Chapter 2.

The main benefits of using styrene are:
- A variety of sheets, some pre-finished ones, strips and sections available in a range of sizes.
- Bonds rapidly with liquid solvent.
- Easy to cut by scoring with a knife and bending until it breaks.
- Clean, smooth surface ready for immediate painting.
- Durable, dimensionally stable and resists warps.
- Compatible with plastic kits and parts.

Figure 9.7 Most model shops carry a stand full of pieces of styrene of various shapes and sizes. (Photo courtesy Evergreen Scale Models)

Figure 9.8 Parts are easily cut from styrene with a craft knife.

You can combine styrene with wood, metal or other plastics using the right adhesives. You can also combine moulded ABS plastic structural shapes with styrene, but again you will need the correct glue. The section below on joining parts contains some useful information about which adhesives are suitable.

Cutting sheets

Styrene sheet is easy to cut by scoring the surface with a sharp craft knife; one light stroke on thin material but several if it is thick. Bend the sheet along the scored line and it will break cleanly with only a slight burr on the edge. Scrape a knife along the edge to remove the burr. You only need cut a quarter-way through the sheet although you can cut right through thin material with several light strokes.

Having cut out openings for doors and windows, you can tidy the corners using a needle file with two adjacent cutting edges.

Cutting strips

Cut styrene strips to length using the same method as for sheets. On thicker strips, score the strip and break to length. This is faster, cleaner and more accurate than sawing. You should, however, cut really heavy sections of styrene with a razor saw or a fine-toothed hacksaw. Do not use a power

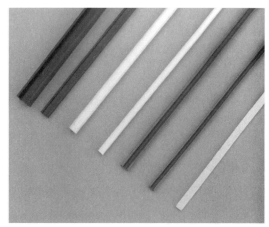

Figure 9.9 Examples of ABS and styrene strip.

saw as the heat from the blade may melt the styrene and jam the blade.

Joining parts

You can join styrene parts by bonding them with the right solvent. To assemble parts, hold them in position and use a small brush or syringe to apply just a little solvent to the joints. Capillary action draws the solvent in, softening the mating surfaces to form a fast bond as strong as the basic material. The more solvent you use, the longer the joint will take to set and the more likely it is

Figure 9.10 Styrene is an easy and flexible material for building models.

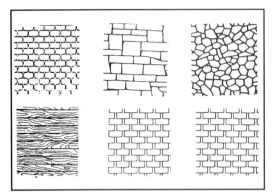

Figure 9.11 Examples of sheet surfaces including brick, stone, crazy paving, wooden planking, slate and tile roofing. (Picture courtesy Peco)

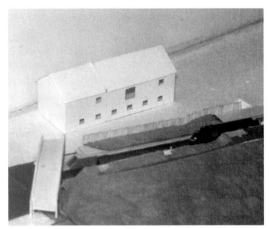

Figure 9.12 A styrene line-side building under construction.

to flow out of the joint. To avoid permanently attaching your model to your work surface, especially when using Micro Weld, Plastic Magic, Plastic Weld or cyano (superglue), do all your gluing on a sheet of polypropylene.

Holding the parts in place for a few seconds while the solvent evaporates, using tweezers for small pieces, results in speedy assembly. On small parts, joints set almost immediately but you do have a few seconds to reposition parts or open up the joint. On larger parts, you can use a syringe to apply the solvent along the joint. This technique is fast, but you should practise it to avoid applying too much solvent. When laminating large parts, use an eyedropper to apply the solvent quickly to both surfaces and press together immediately.

Adhesives

Polystyrene cement, as previously indicated, is not the best adhesive for building plastic kits. It consists of a solvent, usually methyl-based, with some styrene dissolved in it. Liquid solvents, on the other hand, consist solely of the solvent. Cyano glues specially formulated to work with styrene are another alternative and even the standard form works well with metallised parts, gluing them without the need to scrape off the metal coating. These glues are also the only ones that will work with PVC tyres and even then are not that good. Attaching transparent parts can be a problem as the adhesives mentioned above emit fumes which

can cloud the surface. It is better to attach these parts using a small amount of a thinned-down water-based glue, such as a PVA woodworking glue, which dries clear and will not cloud the transparent part.

Styrene to styrene

There are many glues which will bond styrene including liquid plastic cement and a range of proprietary solvent adhesives. Some dry faster than others but the fastest ones do not form the strongest joints. A fast-drying solvent is Methyl Ethyl Ketone (MEK) which is available from most paint suppliers and ironmongers in 500ml containers. However, it is more toxic than the commonly used model solvents making good ventilation even more important.

You cannot glue pre-painted styrene with solvent as it will not work through the paint. Either mask off the edge of a part before painting or scrape it afterwards. You can, however, glue painted styrene with superglue or epoxy.

Hi-impact styrene sheets and strips are more resistant to solvent crazing than the plastic in moulded kits. In addition, some solvents attack the surface of styrene more than others. MEK is the most reactive and will severely craze moulded parts although it works well on styrene sheets and strips. The proprietary solvents seem to cause the least crazing of moulded parts. Do not try to use the thick polystyrene cement from a tube as it is difficult to use, slow to dry and can warp thin styrene sheet.

Styrene to metal or wood

Use gap-filling superglue or epoxy for making strong joints between styrene and wood or metal. Make sure all metal and styrene parts are clean before gluing for maximum joint strength. You can use solvent-free contact adhesive for gluing flat surfaces of styrene to wood.

Painting and decoration

Any plastic must be scrupulously clean prior to painting. This means that you should wash all the parts in warm water with a little washing-up liquid and carefully dry prior to painting. Alternatively wipe them over, using kitchen roll, with a de-greaser like methylated spirits. Either of these methods will remove any grease, including finger prints and also help to minimise any static charge which will attract dust. Probably the biggest

problems in painting and decorating a model lie in avoiding touching the model during painting with what are inevitably greasy fingers and dealing with really small components. These latter are often best painted before detachment from their sprue. You can obtain a superb finish on major items, like a car body, by spraying them with enamel paint.

You can use any type of enamel or acrylic paint on styrene, though matt paints give the best results and you can always varnish them afterwards to protect the finish. When brush painting, select an oil- or water-based paint made for plastic models. Experiment on test pieces if you are unsure of the end result. Consider using more than one type of paint, a basic colour sprayed on, matt enamel for the brush-painted trim, and water-based paints for the weathering. Spray painting provides the best results if the model has a well-maintained gloss finish.

Figure 9.13 Work in hand completing the painting of this model of a Messerschmidt Me 262.

Part 3 – Applications of plastics

The final part of this book examines the use of plastic materials in the many and varied branches of modelling. Just because your own interests lie in a particular area of modelling does not mean that you cannot learn from other sectors.

Good examples include the use of 1/72nd aircraft, built from plastic kits, on the large model aircraft carrier shown below, which regularly takes to the water, and the use of buildings produced for model railways by military modellers and wargamers.

You must also accept that while plastics are brilliant for some applications, they are just not right for others. The aim of this part of the book is to indicate where plastics bring the greatest advantages, whether in ease of construction, minimisation of cost, durability or resistance to the effect of water or other chemicals. Hopefully, you will see the potential of man-made plastics and try your hand at incorporating these materials in your next model, thus gaining the benefits that plastics can bring to your hobby.

This large radio controlled aircraft carrier deck is brought alive by the small styrene aircraft on its deck.

Chapter 10 Flying models

Model aircraft

In the early days of flying model aircraft they were usually built from bamboo, but quickly balsa wood became the staple material with tissue paper or silk covering the open structure and shrunk in place with water and then cellulose dope. It wasn't really until the 1960s that plastics started to appear on the aeromodelling scene in any quantities. Probably the first major application was the use of nylon for propellers and in fabric form to cover control-line and larger radio controlled (R/C) models. This was rapidly followed by the development of heat-shrink self-adhesive covering materials and the provision of a wide range of injection-moulded plastic components, mainly but not exclusively for R/C aircraft. Then came the use of expanded polystyrene foam for wings and other components like fins and tailplanes

Figure 10.1 This simple flying model is made from balsa strip and plastic sheet.

Figure 10.2 A minimum cost, basic free-flight aircraft, made from polystyrene wallpaper backing, provides a perfect introduction to model aircraft.

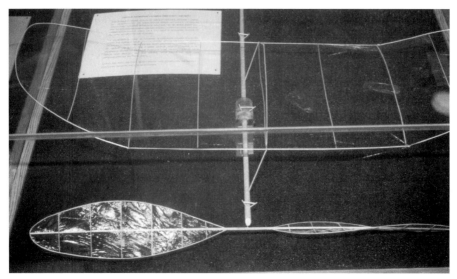

Figure 10.3 It is possible to make an incredibly light-weight indoor flying model covered with microfilm, made by floating cellulose dope on the surface of a bowl of water.

around the same time that GRP and other composite materials began to be seen in significant amounts on models.

Radio control equipment and vibration are unhappy partners and crashes are not good news for the vulnerable electronic equipment. You can protect items like the receiver with foam rubber, and isolate servos and gyros from the worst effects of vibration with synthetic rubber grommets or double-sided servo tape.

Free-flight models are often simply made, with wings from materials as basic as the foam insulation you can put behind wallpaper. Another type of model construction involves sticking a simple balsa frame to a printed plastic sheet covering. There is also an increasing use of expanded polystyrene in smaller models, which has sufficient strength without reinforcement, many of which are described in magazines like ***Aeromodeller***.

Figure 10.4 This radio controlled, ARTF model is almost entirely made from plastics.

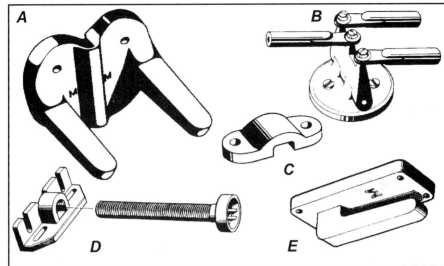

Figure 10.5 A selection of plastic items:
A – Engine mount
B – Control mixer
C – Saddle clamp
D – Wing bolt
E – Tow hook
(Pictures courtesy Chart)

Plastic models

Today, there are some models made virtually entirely from plastic, particularly those which are almost-ready-to-fly (ARTF) like the Aircore 40, which are well able to survive crashes that would destroy a conventionally built wooden model.

There is also a growing number of model kits and plans using increasing amounts of plastic sheet like Corex in their construction, allied to veneered foam wings. Corex is a very pliable material which you can easily fold to make a box structure and readily glue with contact adhesive or cyano. It is also relatively indestructible compared with conventional wooden materials. It is clear that this trend will continue as designers and builders become more familiar with the benefits.

Ancillary items

Many ancillary items are made from plastic, usually injection moulded, and these have the widest possible application for model aircraft, particularly radio controlled ones. Other items you can make yourself from scrap plastic.

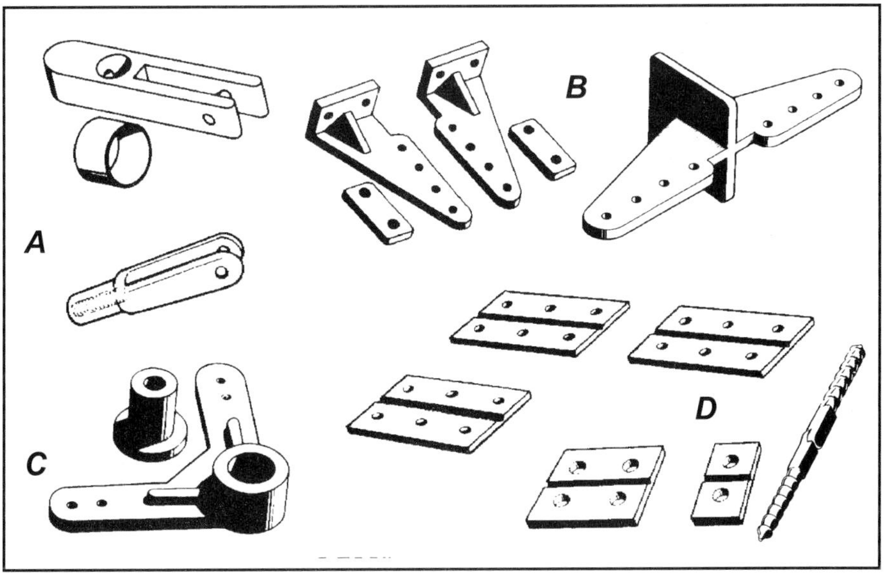

Figure 10.6 More components made from plastic:
A – Clevises
B – Horns
C – Bell-crank
D – Hinges
(Pictures courtesy Chart)

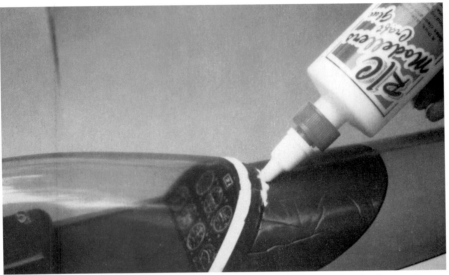

Figure 10.7 It is always difficult to glue a canopy neatly in place. R/C Modellers glue dries transparent and is ideal for the task. (Photo courtesy Deluxe Materials)

Glass-reinforced nylon is the popular material for propellers for internal-combustion engined model aircraft, though some are plain nylon and others of carbon fibre-reinforced nylon. It is also widely used for engine mounts.

Most other R/C accessories such as horns, clevises, bell-cranks and spinners are also made from nylon. Bubble canopies are readily vacuum formed from clear acetate or butyrate sheet. You can form cowls, wing tips and wheel spats from ABS, though you may prefer GRP for larger and tougher items. Wheels are made from a range of plastics. Nylon is the preferred material for the hub, but the tyres may be from synthetic rubber or, when air filled, moulded PVC. It is easy to make your own tyres from suitable black tube joined with cyano.

Fuel tanks are usually transparent polythene when used for glow fuel. You will find you can convert many discarded polythene containers for this role. When connecting the tank to the engine, silicone rubber tubing is perfect, but for diesel or petrol, you must use neoprene tubing instead. Neoprene is also usable with glow fuel.

Figure 10.8 Covering an open-structure wing or tail surface requires the use of plastic unless you choose tissue or silk. This one uses Solarfilm.

For servo linkages to the control surfaces on R/C models, a mixture of metal and plastic is widespread. Hinges, clevises and horns are either entirely made from plastic or metal and plastic. Flexible hinges may be mylar or polypropylene, while two-part hinges are usually nylon. This gives rise to difficulties with adhesion and painting. The extent of the problem depends on the actual plastic involved. Chapters 3 and 4 gives more information on these subjects.

Covering materials

A wide range of materials is available to cover open structures, such as wings and tail surfaces, and to add strength to sheeted components like fuselages. The choice of plastic-based coverings divides basically into nylon on the one hand and the many varied self-adhesive custom-made films and textured coverings on the other.

Nylon

Since the boom in popularity of free-flight and control-line aeromodelling in the 1950s, the use

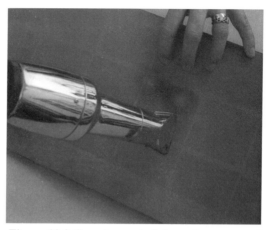

Figure 10.9 *Covering materials are best tautened using a heat gun.*

of nylon to cover the wings of model aircraft, or even the complete airframe, has provided a really tough hard-wearing solution. Applied wet, attached with cellulose dope and pinned firmly in place, the nylon will dry to a taut, tough

' I DIDN'T THINK PLASTICS WERE THAT HEAT SENSITIVE ! '

Figure 10.10 Self-adhesive instruments should improve the look of your model's cockpit.

covering ready for the application of further coats of clear dope to make the material airtight. This is then followed by painting and final decoration to choice and usually a coating of fuel-proofer.

Films

A problem, when covering a wing using dope is the extremely strong smell. This was one of the factors which led to the provision of iron-on self-adhesive plastic coverings, now supplied in an ever widening choice of colours and properties.

Most of these materials are backed with a heat-sensitive glue, allowing you to stick them in place with an iron and then tauten them with the iron or a heat gun. There is more information about using these techniques in Chapter 5.

Textured coverings

As well as smooth film coverings, there are also textured materials which simulate the linen used to cover all early full-size aircraft and still found on a number of light aircraft. These coverings

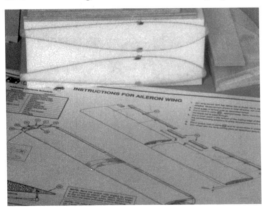

Figure 10.11 The veneered foam wings for the Flair Cub, straight out of the kit box, protected by the offcuts.

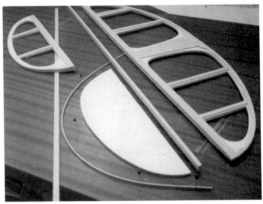

Figure 10.12 Building all the tail surfaces from foam board is an easy task. (Photo courtesy Paper Aviation)

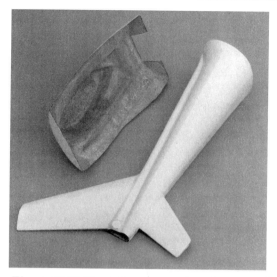

Figure 10.13 The tail section and top housing of a GRP helicopter fuselage.

Figure 10.14 A glass-reinforced nylon ducted fan unit and outer duct section.

are generally tougher and more puncture resistant than films, but tend to be rather heavier. There is a list of plastic covering materials in Table 5.1 on page 55.

Decoration

Most model aircraft require decorating, if only to improve visibility in the air. Scale models try to replicate their full-size prototypes. Thus self-coloured covering materials, paints, varnishes and self-adhesive sheet all have their place. Roundels, lettering and instrument panels are all available printed on self-adhesive vinyl sheet. Important considerations are the weight of these finishes, their adhesive powers, their immunity from chemical attack between layers and their durability. Plastic materials are better in most respects than others.

Foam components

Wings

The use of expanded polystyrene to make wing cores for aircraft is increasingly popular to due the speed and simplicity of construction allied to only a minor weight penalty. Complex aerofoil sections present little difficulty and it is easy to vary the aerofoil from root to tip. Chapter 8 explains how to cut components like wing cores from expanded polystyrene. It is normal practice

to join veneer-covered foam wings with GRP tape well soaked in resin.

It is often said that more models suffer from hanger rash (damage on the ground) than are ever damaged when flying. Whether this is true or not, you can easily protect your wing from damage during transit by making a wing bag from transparent bubble-wrap sheeting.

Composite components

For scale models, particularly jets, gliders and for some sports aircraft, there are signs of increasing use of GRP fuselages and, in some cases, wings and tail surfaces as well. Such fuselages retain their shape well with a minimum of internal support and it is relatively straightforward to build in considerable surface detail such as panel lines and rows of rivets.

Smaller items like cowls and even undercarriage legs benefit from being made from GRP. For additional strength, carbon fibre reinforcement is popular, for example along the main spar of glider wings.

You can also use small amounts of chopped strand mat, stuck in place with GRP resin, to strengthen vulnerable internal and external parts of built-up wooden structures. Chapter 7 shows you how to make items from GRP and other composite materials.

Figure 10.15 Radio control-led helicopters make a lot of use of plastics in their con-struction.

Ducted fans and turbojets

The actual fans used in flying ducted fan jet mod-els are usually moulded from glass-reinforced nylon and an increasing number of people are making fans themselves, particularly for electric-powered models, using plastic sheeting for the blades. More advanced home builders construct-ing Kurt Schrekling's FD3/64 working model turbojet have discovered that it features a ply-wood compressor reinforced with carbon fibres embedded in epoxy resin.

Radio controlled helicopters

Modern radio controlled helicopters are increas-ingly dependent on the use of plastic for their construction and their relatively low cost. From carbon-reinforced rotor-head components to polycarbonate cockpit housings, plastics are an integral part of any helicopter.

Scale models almost invariably enclose a set of standard mechanical components within a GRP

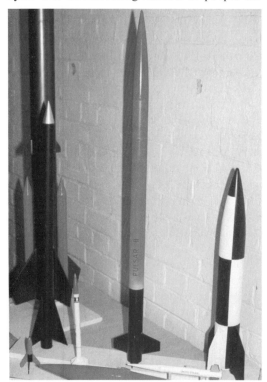

Figure 10.16 Model rockets come in a range of sizes, often making extensive use of plastics for fuselages and nose cones.

Figure 10.17 Fixing terylene chord to a polythene rocket chute requires a careful choice of adhe-sive. (Photo courtesy Deluxe Materials)

Figure 10.18 Helium-filled airships almost invariably use either mylar or melinex sheet to form the envelope.

fuselage and polycarbonate cockpit. Care is needed when you are constructing and decorating these models to make sure you follow the manufacturer's instructions in terms of adhesives, final decorative paints and any self-adhesive materials.

Model rockets

The flying model rockets, pioneered by Estes, are powered by solid-fuel motors. The kits contain many plastic parts, including the main parachute as well as self-adhesive decals. Weight is always a problem so that thin plastic tubes and pre-shaped nose cones are popular. You can make a fuselage yourself from very thin GRP or carbon fibre composites.

An entirely different propulsion system uses the expulsion of water under pressure from a plastic (polyester) bottle; the airspace in the bottle being pressurised with a bicycle pump. The nozzle and fins are generally injection-moulded items. Again, you can make your own rockets using an empty polyester drinks bottle with styrene sheet fins.

Parachutes

Plastic is the ideal material for simple lightweight chutes which are inexpensive. The ones that come in kits are pre-printed, usually with alternate red and white panels. You can easily make your own from thin polythene sheet. Terylene or nylon chords provide adequate strength combined with light weight and you can glue the lines to the chute with acrylic glue.

Balloons and airships

Mylar or melinex, in thin sheet form, is an ideal material for making hot-air balloons. The advantage of these materials is their low weight (as low as 10gsm) and excellent maintenance of shape, despite being quite flimsy. They are the materials used for helium-filled balloons and airships as their closely spaced molecules leave insufficient space between for helium, itself a small molecule, to pass through. Despite this, there will still be a gradual helium loss.

You can glue these plastics or heat-seal them to provide an airtight envelope. A few airships and balloons have used vinyl envelopes, but this material is not recommended.

For hot-air balloons, you can also use lightweight nylon or terylene cloth, carefully stitching the panels together to form the envelope. These materials are normally self-coloured and do not require further finishing. Clearly, mylar or melinex sheet is the most airtight and, when the joins are heat-sealed, results in the lightest

Figure 10.19 A kite like this uses little but plastic, in a variety of forms, in its construction.

envelope. In all cases, suspension cords made from nylon or terylene are normal.

Kites

Some people are surprised to discover that you can build a full-size kite entirely from plastic materials and end up with a cost-effective, high-performance flying machine.

A kite basically consists of four components; the frame, the covering material, the rigging and tow line, and the tail. While you can make the frame from wooden strip or metal rod, the best strength/weight ratio comes from a composite material like carbon fibre. Other types of rod, made from the stiffer plastics, also provide satisfactory strength-to-weight ratios.

The covering is more resistant to damp and dirt if made from rip-stop nylon or terylene, while the rigging and tow line are almost invariably from one of these two plastics. You can equally well use polythene sheet for the covering; either transparent or self-coloured.

Whether you sew the covering to the frame, glue it or use self-adhesive tape will vary depending on your choice of covering and personal inclination.

What is important is to choose compatible materials if you decide on adhesive or tape. The tail also lends itself to being made from a length of plastic tape; again polythene is a good choice and will not fray.

Chapter 11 Ships and boats

Model boats

Models of ships or boats, which operate on or below the surface of water, all offer opportunities for the use of plastics in their construction. They come in all shapes and sizes. Powered craft, whether steam, internal-combustion engine or electric powered, sailing boats and submarines all have their followings, both radio controlled and free sailing.

While wood always used to be the traditional construction material, this has largely been replaced by one or another type of plastic, at least for the hulls of all but scale ships of the pre-steam era.

Hulls and fittings

Popular materials for making boat hulls include ABS, vacuum formed to shape, and GRP built in a mould. Wooden hulls are often coated with resin to improve impact resistance. For ultimate strength, you could build a complete hull from carbon fibre but, due to its cost, it is more popular for highly stressed components like yacht masts and decks.

It is also a useful material for adding local strength where it is most needed. However, you will need local reinforcement where carbon fibre parts are drilled for hooks and fittings to avoid splitting. In the same way, you can use kevlar to reinforce hulls and yacht fins where they are subject to heavy stress.

For powered models, you can make long-lasting bearings from Nylatron GS or PTFE, both of which have very low coefficients of friction.

Figure 11.1 Not, perhaps, a typical model boat, the Robbe Sea Jet is electric powered and is supplied with a vacuum-formed hull.

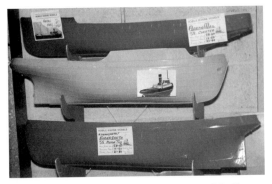

Figure 10.2 Ready made GRP or ABS hulls are impervious to water and significantly reduce hull construction time. These are some of the wide variety offered at most model shows.

Synthetic rubber O-ring seals will help to prevent the ingress of water, while you can custom-build seals between superstructure and deck from silicone rubber. Glass-reinforced nylon is a popular material for propellers. It is cheaper and lighter than brass and also better able to resist attack by the corrosive effects of salt water.

In order to try to make your boat unsinkable, you can fill voids in the hull with polyester foam which will expand to fill the free space. Do not, however, overdo the initial filling as the foam continues to expand as it cures. Rubber fenders are usually made from synthetic rubber but you can also cast your own from silicone rubber, coloured with aniline black.

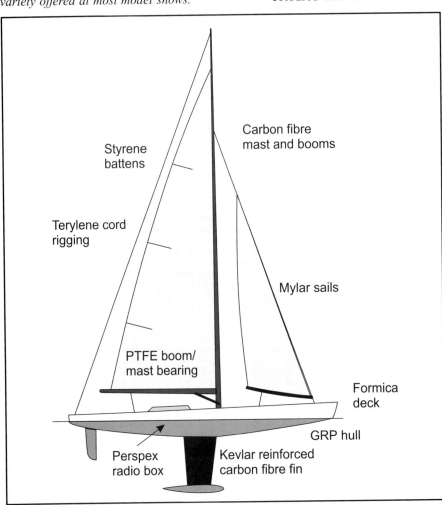

Figure 11.3 A typical radio controlled model yacht showing the extensive possible use of plastics.

Yacht sails

The advantage of making your sails from man-made materials is their long life and their speed of drying out after getting wet. Materials such as terylene and nylon are popular. The elasticity of nylon makes it ideal for spinnakers.

For mainsails, jibs and other foresails, terylene is probably the most popular material. Useful weights range up to 50gsm for the smallest sails and 75gsm or more for larger vessels. You can choose different size threads at right angles to each other – the warp and weft – for sailcloth. In addition, you can easily dye your sails to your preferred colour or just buy coloured material. Stitched with man-made thread, these sails will last a lifetime.

Laminated sails

The problem with using sails made from woven materials is their lack of stretch resistance on the bias (diagonally to the weave). This can be overcome by using mylar or melinex, which are laminated, stretch- and tear-resistant materials. The advantage of these materials is their low weight and better maintenance of shape compared to woven materials. They do, however, appear

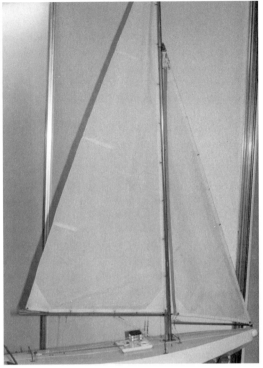

Figure 11.4 Sails and rigging are good areas to use the right plastic materials.

' I THOUGHT THIS CAN WOULD CONTAIN JUST ENOUGH TO FILL THE BOAT !'

Figure 11.5 Unconventional models, like this duck and ducklings, benefit from the use of plastics, particularly for cloning the ducklings.

more transparent and flimsy. Mylar and melinex are available in weights from 10gsm upwards.

Rigging

Terylene in the form of woven cord is ideal for rigging, sheeting and the like due to its resistance to stretching and its ability to emulate the texture of rope. Monofilament nylon or nylon-covered fishing trace, depending on the scale of the model, are better for simulating cables running to aerials.

Superstructure

It is important to keep topside weight as low as possible and, in many ways, styrene plastic sheet

is a better material than plywood, due to the latter's susceptibility to warping in the presence of damp. Plastic sheet cuts and breaks cleanly and easily and does not tear along the grain when cut. It is easy to make openings for portholes and hatches and rivets are simple to simulate.

You can make decks from corex, GRP, ABS, styrene sheet and, in the case of some boats such as yachts and speed boats, even from heat-shrink materials like Solartex. For the more flexible of these materials, you must have a supporting structure.

Fittings and decoration

While there is a huge range of ready-made fittings, you can always cast your own. This can prove economical, particularly if you need a large number of a particular item. Chapter 6 shows how to make silicone rubber moulds and Chapter 7 explains how to work with casting resin.

Many hulls are self-finishing plastics like ABS and GRP, while wooden hulls need the protection of modern paints and/or varnishes. You will normally have to paint the superstructure as well, with transparent plastic sheeting filling portholes and windows. Self-adhesive vinyl decals or rub-down lettering help to improve realism.

Radio control

The electronics of radio control and water really do not mix well. Even dampness in the radio can

Figure 11.6 HM Customs Cutter Sentinel, under construction by Mick Bond, has a hull of GRP and superstructure cut from printed styrene sheet.

easily cause a malfunction, usually at the worse possible moment. You can buy special plastic boxes and install your radio inside. These boxes come complete with transparent perspex lid and self-adhesive foam seals for the lid, easy access to the radio switch and crystal as well as synthetic rubber bellows to accommodate the servo outputs.

The use of plastics for all these various parts helps to ensure the radio equipment inside is kept perfectly dry at an affordable price. You can equally easily make your own radio container from a suitably-sized resealable food box or other plastic box, forming your own seals from silicone rubber.

Waterproof seals

Plastics are the only really practical way of making waterproof seals, whether their purpose is to seal the hull to the deck, keep radio equipment waterproof or to seal a gland on a prop shaft or control run.

For sealing the deck to the hull, there are two possible approaches. Either you can stick a self-adhesive seal in place or you can cast your own custom seal from silicone rubber. Circular seals and glands are easily made from proprietary synthetic rubber O-rings or seals.

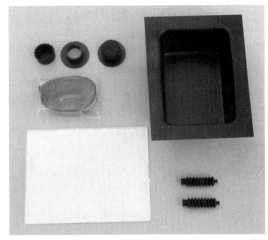

Figure 11.7 This container for housing radio equipment includes an ABS box, perspex lid, foam seal and synthetic rubber caps and bellows.

Submarines

Vessels which sail underwater present special problems for the builder, at least some of which are considerably simplified by the availability of a range of plastic materials. Modern nuclear powered boats are readily scratch built using a length of 100mm PVC soil pipe as the main hull. Otherwise, as Figure 11.11 overleaf shows, you can use a sealed acrylic pipe, inside the main hull,

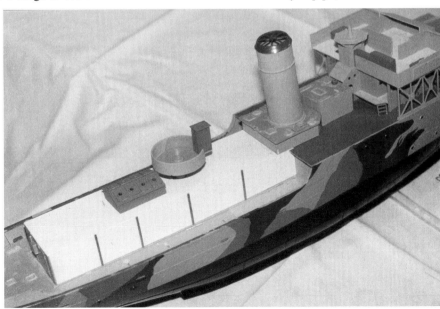

Figure 11.8 Extensive use is made of sheet styrene in the super-structure of this model to keep top-side weight to a minimum.

Figure 11.9 The removable deck of a working submarine made from styrene sheet with supports held in place using epoxy putty.

Figure 11.10 A hovercraft is reliant on a plastic skirt for operation.

to house the radio and other electrical equipment. Access can either be from each end using large O-ring seals or, if the hull cross-section is not circular, by screwing down a perspex hatch on a custom-made silicone rubber main seal.

You can access the radio and main power switches via a small soil pipe stop-end glued to the hull, while connections from any radio to external control surfaces generally use rubber bellows. An O-ring on the prop shaft will stop water ingress via this route.

Hovercraft

It is a questionable whether a hovercraft should be classified as a flying model, a ship or a land vehicle. In no doubt is the need for plastics in its construction, primarily in its skirts, but also in most other areas. Examples include GRP for the hull and styrene for the superstructure. Soft vinyl sheet is probably one of the best materials for making the skirt, though synthetic rubber sheet can prove equally practical.

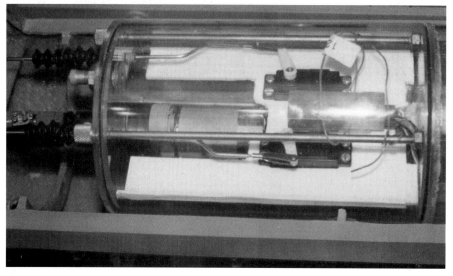

Figure 11.11 This submarine hull interior, made from acrylic is kept water tight with O-ring seals at each end and synthetic rubber bellows for the control rods exits.

Chapter 12 Cars and land vehicles

Model cars

There are two distinct categories of working cars, apart from the wide range of other freelance working models. The first is the ubiquitous radio controlled car, whether it is a four-wheel drive off-the-road vehicle or an out-and-out racing sports car, regardless of whether it is powered by an internal-combustion engine or an electric motor. The other is the much smaller electric-powered slot car, popularised by Scalectrix.

There is a considerable following for trams, used in a similar fashion to model trains, as well as a number of individually crafted cars. Included in Chapter 15 are steam-powered vehicles which are truly model engineering subjects.

On the static side, there is an even larger variation. The tiniest size are resin-cast models as accessories to the smallest gauge model railways. Then there are custom-built models of cars, using bodies made from styrene sheet, or formed from materials like ABS or GRP, in a variety of sizes. Finally there are the various horse-drawn carriages and wagons which, although mostly made from wood, still benefit from the occasional use of plastic.

R/C cars

Powered model cars, whether radio controlled or not, live a hectic life and have to endure regular crashes. Many people start radio controlled model car racing at a young age and this competitive sport has a large following. Bodies from Lexan, a polycarbonate, or GRP are immensely strong and readily decorated to meet the finishes seen on full-size cars. The problem of painting and

Figure 12.1 A classic R/C model sports car that is built mainly from a range of plastic materials.

Figure 12.2 These beautiful miniatures are resin cast to 2mm scale. (Photo courtesy Cedric Verdon)

decorating Lexan is that many paints and glues attack the plastic and make it brittle. Take care, therefore, and always use Lexan/polycarbonate compatible paints. These are mostly acrylic-based and need compatible thinners as well. It is not difficult to make your own car body if you follow the instructions given in Chapter 5 for vacuum forming or Chapter 7 for composites.

You can now purchase or make foam body protectors to preserve your immaculate body finish. Injection-moulded items like mirrors, windscreen wipers, rear wings and aerials add to the realism of most models or you can make your own from styrene sheet, other scraps of plastic or cast them from epoxy.

Chassis items

The immense strength of carbon fibre composites is making them an increasingly popular replacement for GRP as the chassis of an R/C car. This composite is so tough that it can help if you lubricate screws before fixing them in place. Suspension arms are normally made from glass

Figure 12.3 This classic early Reliant 3-wheeler uses plastic for glazing and tyres.

Figure 12.4 A polycarbonate car body before painting. The windows are often left clear.

Figure 12.5 A carbon fibre chassis plate is the basis of this battery-powered car. Note also the nylon tie-wraps holding the battery in place.

Figure 12.6 Plastic wheel hubs can match almost any full-size pattern.

reinforced plastics, while plastic-toothed belts are frequently found in the transmission chain. The resilience of nylon makes it an ideal bumper material and it is also useful for making items like wings.

Tyres and tracks
Tyres are available in quite a range of different compositions of synthetic rubber to provide varying degrees of softness, not to mention slicks and treaded, wet-weather tyres. There is also a growing following for tracked vehicles, anything from a snowcat to a tank. Here, the track itself is almost invariably made from one of the synthetic rubbers, unless the construction of individual metal links is attempted.

'*I THOUGHT THE PAINT I WAS USING WAS OK ON POLYCARBONATE!*'

Figure 12.7 As with full-size practice, synthetic rubber is widely used to make model car tyres.

Freelance working models

If you scratch-build a working vehicle, apart from making your own plastic bodywork from a mould, you can build one from styrene sheet if the original prototype is fairly angular. You will usually want to provide clear glazing from acetate or butyrate sheet, though you may fashion the various lights from suitably coloured perspex. You can fabricate tyres from blackened silicone rubber and a single mould will reduce the effort of making five identical tyres; four plus a spare.

Figure 12.9 Plastic caterpillar tracks come in a wide range of sizes and are ideal for models of tanks, bulldozers and rough-terrain vehicles.

Figure 12.8 A carbon fibre chassis plate and numerous plastic suspension parts.

Electric slot cars

The electric slot-racing car is very different from an R/C car with its special track providing guidance and electric power to each car. Race tracks are mainly based on the popular Scalectrix plastic base with metal-lined conductor slots.

The cars are mostly injection moulded; both body and chassis. You can readily make your own, using plastic sheet, heat or vacuum formed to shape, as well as by fabricating them from GRP. In both cases, you will have to make your own

Figure 12.10 There are a few radio controlled motorbikes, but the vast majority of models of these machines are static ones.

Figure 12.11
There are few parts in a slot car that are not made from plastic.

original form and, in the case of GRP a female mould as well.

Motorcycles

Because of balance problems, almost all bike models are static ones, although there has been the odd radio controlled one. The static ones use plastics extensively, usually styrene, both coloured and clear, for all the components except for the tyres which may be of PVC or synthetic rubber. Making your own radio controlled model requires the use of a rather tougher material and GRP is

probably the best for replicating the various formed metal parts.

Trams

An unusual mixture of train and road vehicle, model trams are usually associated with the era before 1950 when they were very widely used for public transport within large towns and cities. More recently, new-style trams are being re-introduced in a number of British cities and their modern shape lends itself to moulding from a suitable plastic.

Figure 12.12
A slot car track usually includes many plastic items such as scatter materials, trees, hedges and figures. There is more information on this subject in Chapter 13.

Figure 12.13 A tram needs clear windows and insulators for its electric drive system.

Regardless of the period and scale, the use of some form of plastic within the construction of any tram is virtually essential to reproduce the extensive glazing. At the smallest sizes, you can cast complete trams from clear resin or make them from styrene sheet and strip. As the scale increases, the use of GRP is useful for simulating complex metal parts.

Carriages, caravans and carts

While, in larger scales, these vehicles are almost exclusively made from wood, apart from replicas of modern caravans, again acetate glazing is normal and you may find synthetic substitutes for making harnesses and upholstery better than the original materials like leather and cloth.

Whenever the wheels are fitted with rubber tyres, a synthetic alternative is ideal and readily custom made and glued in place. In the smaller scales, resin casting is again an option as is the use of built-up construction from styrene materials.

Figure 12.14 A beautiful carriage like this one is mainly made from natural materials, but plastics may creep into parts like the hood, wheels and uphol-stery.

Chapter 13 Buildings and layouts

Buildings

Any sort of building made from plastic may come complete and painted or as a kit which you can build to plan or modify. In addition, many people choose to scratch build from wood, plastic or a mixture of both.

Styrene is the most common material for model building construction and there is a wide and varying range of architectural sections and components. These parts come as white styrene structural shapes and also grey ABS and white butyrate tubing and fittings. Items include angles, beams, channels and girders. Whether you are making a building for a railway layout working in 1/72nd scale or a doll's house at 1/12th scale, this range of materials is ideal.

Some manufacturers produce embossed and coloured brick for walls from styrene. A few can even provide arches in the brickwork from

expanded polystyrene which minimises weight on portable layouts. This is in addition to a wide range of 4mm styrene sheets of boarding, bricks, cement rendering, clapboard, cobblestones, concrete blocks, corrugated asbestos and iron, paving, slates, stones and tiles.

Smaller-scale buildings are increasingly made almost entirely from plastics, using styrene sheet for the walls and roof with clear acetate for the glazing.

At larger scales, foam board is particularly useful because of its rigidity. You can make smaller items, such as window sills and door frames, from styrene, which you can easily glue in place. Transparent acetate or butyrate sheet is the perfect material for glazing the windows.

You can even remove one skin of foam board and scribe and texture the revealed foam surface. Pre-formed hand rails and stair rails in OO and

Figure 13.1 A typical scene from a narrow-gauge railway layout. (Photo courtesy Evergreen Plastics)

N gauge help to increase realism for a minimum expenditure of time when creating a station.

At the smallest sizes, you can resin-cast complete buildings, a technique which is particularly useful if you require a number of identical houses.

Working styrene
Surface finish

If you want to simulate wood grain or similar surface effects, you should do this before cutting the parts to size. You can achieve a light or medium wood-grain effect by rubbing styrene sheet or strips in a single direction with medium or coarse sandpaper. You can add knots with the teeth of a razor saw and very coarse sandpaper, removing any raised styrene with fine sandpaper and marking nail holes with a sharp scriber. You can randomly score prepared strips to simulate individual planks. When constructing brick or stone buildings, you can use the appropriately embossed sheet, while plain sheet suffices for rendered or concrete surfaces.

Reinforce the inside corners of your buildings with square strips. A reasonably thick ceiling, permanently glued in place, will brace the walls and keep the corners square. Removable floors provide access to the interior for detailing and painting. Hold the floors in place with strips glued to the inside of the walls at the floor level.

Windows and door holes

Window and door openings are straightforward to cut in styrene. The basic score and break method works well on material up to 1mm thick, providing the opening is not near the edge of the sheet. Simply score deeply, using several passes and carefully flex the opening on all four sides. For openings near to the edge of a piece of styrene sheet, drill a pilot hole and saw out the opening with a fine piercing saw. A needle file with two smooth edges is ideal for making square corners. Since styrene has no grain, there is little risk of splitting the material even when cutting close to an edge.

Roofs

You can use embossed sheet to simulate tiles or slates but if you want individual tiles, stick them to a sub-roof prior to attaching the whole panel in place. Install the roof and roof trim before

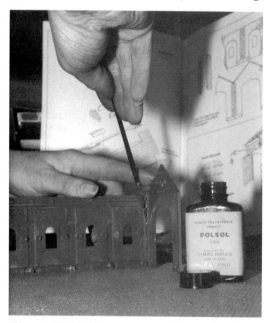

Figure 13.2 *Gluing parts together with solvent. (Photo courtesy Peco)*

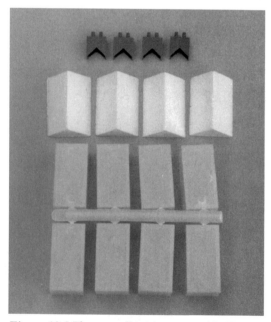

Figure 13.3 *These small injection-moulded houses have expanded polystyrene roofs.*

Figure 13.4 A layout with resin-cast buildings before and after painting.

Figure 13.5 It is normal to use pre-printed acetate glazing for the windows of smaller-scale buildings.

painting to provide a strong styrene-to-styrene bond. Roofing with individual tiles representing slate, clay or concrete provides a most realistic result and is simple, if time consuming, to achieve. Using thin styrene sheet, cut strips the scale height of the tiles and then slice the strips to length. Draw lines on the sub-roof about half a tile height apart. Pick up the tiles with a sharp needle and set in place. Cement along the top edge only, using a very small amount of solvent.

Dolls' houses

A dolls' house is something of a specialist building and is often subject to considerable handling of items in its interior. Dolls' houses are traditionally built robustly from plywood, but fittings like doors and windows, though often made of wood, are readily purchased at a significantly lower cost as plastic mouldings. If you are happy with the colour of the plastic, usually white, then these fittings do not even need painting.

Figure 13.5 Any type of dolls' house requires the use of plastic in its construction, if only for the windows.

Figure 13.6 The white door and windows in this illustration are made from plastic, whereas the darker ones are wooden, normally with plastic glazing. (Photo courtesy Dolls' House Emporium)

Acetate sheet is the norm for glazing regardless of whether the windows themselves are wooden or plastic. In fact, there is often a surprising amount of plastic in any dolls' house. It is worth examining two major classes of dolls' house; those designed for children and those restricted to adult use only. The latter are less likely to use plastics except where plastics are used in the full-sized prototype. For the child, plastic furniture and crockery are commonplace.

Resin-cast items can range from simple grates and fireplaces to more elaborate ones with glowing coals. The technique, covered in detail in Chapter 7, is equally applicable to the home production of radiators, light switches and power sockets as it is to baths, wash basins, sinks and WCs.

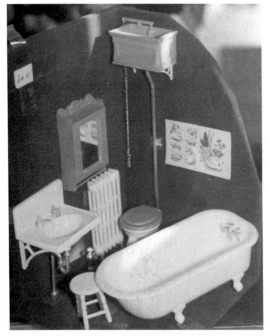

Figure 13.7 Bathroom furniture lends itself to the resin-casting process with additives to provide a self-coloured finish.

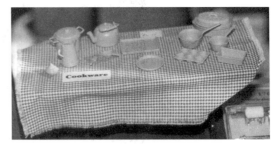

Figure 13.8 Crockery and kitchenware are readily formed at home from thermoplastics or cast from resin.

Figure 13.9 This charming ironmonger's shop shows how a range of natural and plastic materials can sit in harmony.

You can find an amazing range of plastic fittings for dolls' houses including front and interior doors and door frames, single, double and treble plain, lattice, Georgian and Victorian windows both sash and swing opening, window sills, shutters, fireplaces, staircases, banisters, pediments, dentils, quoins, soldier arches and chimneys. Some items, like the lampshades shown in Figure 13.10 mimic the original items in their use of plastics and you can readily cast them yourself from clear resin..

While many people concentrate on creating the past in their dolls' houses, anyone creating a replica of the period post-1970 will face having to model the increasing amount of plastic found in the full-size prototype. This is where styrene proves invaluable for custom-building small items like plastic-seated dining chairs and garden tables.

Single rooms are also a popular area for dolls' house enthusiasts and allow an even wider choice of subjects, as the shop front in Figure 13.9 shows. Again the judicious use of plastic materials brings many advantages.

Gardens for dolls' houses differ little from other scenic layouts, except that the scale is often larger. Details are provided later in this chapter about the use of scatter materials, trees and other natural features.

Layouts

Modelling the landscape is a common need for military modelling, construction of model railways

Figure 13.10 A pair of delightful Tiffany light shades in polyester resin. They are not difficult to make and are easily decorated with acrylic paints.

Figure 13.11
There is plenty of plastic in sight on this layout including various roofs, doors and windows.

in the smaller scales – O gauge and below – as well as in wargaming. It is also necessary in dealing with smaller areas for dolls' house gardens and dioramas. In all cases a firm wooden baseboard is employed, but it is what goes on top of this that is of interest here. Particularly popular for its light weight and the ease with which you can carve it is expanded polystyrene. You do, however, need to seal the surface, which is easily done with emulsion paint.

Scatter materials

To provide the correct texture and colouring, there is a wide choice of scatter materials. The naturally occurring ones, such as sand and granite chippings, tend to suffer from extensive weight. Plastic scatter materials abound and allow you to model any scene from country pasture to town centre in any of the four seasons. Different coloured materials simulate various types of grass and flowers, different earths and road surfaces as

Figure 13.12
Special glues are available for attaching scatter materials to baseboards. (Photo courtesy Deluxe Materials)

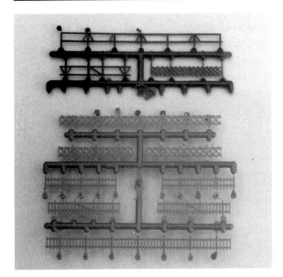

Figure 13.13 *Plastic fences and plastic stone walls also help you to add realism to rural areas.*

Figure 13.14 *You can make trees for layouts and cover them with plastic scatter material.*

well as railway ballast. Likewise, ready-made plastic-based trees and flexible hedging can help to bring a baseboard to life.

Water

There are several ways of simulating a pond, lake, stream or river from plastic materials. You can fill an appropriately sized and decorated indentation with clear resin, you can paint over a

number of layers of varnish or you can use a piece of transparent ripple plastic suspended over the bed. All provide a realistic result.

Trees and plants

You can purchase plastic trees and hedges ready to fit, but they are expensive if you require any significant quantity. You can make your own from a variety of materials including lichen, string, wire, plastic-coated wire and scatter materials. These last are glued in place with thinned PVA

*Figure 13.15
A totally real-
istic river
scene. (Photo
courtesy Cedric
Verdon)*

Figure 13.16 This exquisite 2mm scale Southern P class locomotive is built from a home-made resin casting. (Photo courtesy Cedric Verdon)

white glue and make realistic foliage economic and straightforward to create.

Model railways

Chapter 15 gives details of the use of plastics in those railway locomotives which are usually of

Figure 13.17 The use of plastic bodies for truck and carriage bodies simplifies additions and modifications using plastics parts.

larger gauge, generally steam powered and are part of the endeavours of the model engineering fraternity. The concentration is on the construction of the locomotive and the question of scenic detail takes a firm second place. Smaller scale electric-powered model railways usually run through both rugged terrain and rolling countryside as well as through urban and industrial areas. Rocky ground is particularly popular with narrow gauge modellers. You can purchase tunnel

Figure 13.18 Regardless of the scale of your layout, plastic materials will form an integral part.

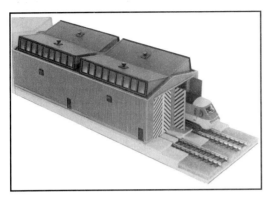

Figure 13.19 This modular plastic engine shed can be built up to a large facility. (Photo courtesy Peco)

entrances and viaducts already pre-moulded in plastic. You can also use plastic sheet for stone lined cuttings and embankments. Alternatively, you can make your own moulds and cast them from resin or fabricate them from GRP.

Locomotives and rolling stock

The vast majority of the railway modelling fraternity work at OO or slightly less commonly at N gauge. O and Z gauges also have their following. OO and N gauge locomotives, passenger and freight carriages and wagons are often made with plastic bodies and a mixture of plastic and metal in their chassis.

Many railway modellers are happy to design their layouts around ready-to-run engines and rolling stock. The use of plastics in these models becomes of much more interest to those who scratch-build or customise their own models. At the top level, etched brass materials are the first choice. However, many are built from styrene

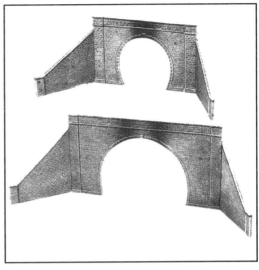

Figure 13.20 Ready-made tunnel mouths certainly speed up building. (Photo courtesy Peco)

sheet and strip, which you can also use to alter ready-to-run models. You can successfully use resin to cast locomotive and carriage bodies in the smaller gauges.

Rivets

Styrene is ideal when making models of riveted and welded metal prototypes. You can use 0.25mm (0.010") or 0.4mm (0.015") sheets for most scales but 0.5mm (.020") stock for larger rivets. You need only very light pressure when using a rivet punch and you should round its end to avoid punching right through the plastic.

Figure 13.21 Platforms, ramps and an arched brick wall, all made from plastic. (Photo courtesy Peco)

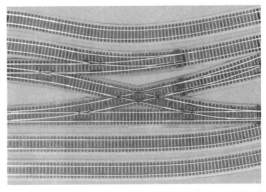

Figure 13.22 Streamline track which has moulded plastic sleepers, here fitted with foam ballast inlay. (Photo courtesy Peco)

117

Track and track bed

While railway lines are most commonly made from nickel steel, the sleepers are almost invariably plastic representations of wood or concrete in scales up to O gauge and in the smallest scales, the ballast may also be a plastic scatter material, particularly if the weight of real granite chipping is likely to cause problems. Ballast, granite or plastic is best held in place with PVA glue diluted with an equal amount of water. It dries completely transparent and will hold the ballast securely in place.

Peco also make moulded foam ballast inlay, already realistically coloured and in rolls for each track and specially moulded to suit turnouts and crossings. Ready-moulded foam underlay is a popular and lightweight solution which also helps to dampen noise. Insulated fishplates are invariable made from plastic, usually nylon.

Line-side accessories

Kits for line-side items are mostly made either from wood, thin card or plastic. Moulded plastic items, such as viaducts and platform edging are enormous time savers.

Depending on the scale, some items are cast from resin but the vast majority are injection moulded. Moulded fencing is so delicate in the smaller gauges that it would be all but impossible and intensely time consuming to produce at home. To avoid your layout looking like anyone else's, you can construct your own accessories from styrene, GRP or casting resin.

Wargaming

The scenario for land warfare may be flat, mountainous, jungle, desert or urban, while seas and coastlines are needed for naval gaming. The time of year may be winter with or without a snow covering, spring, summer or autumn. All these variances affect the way in which you make the baseboard. Hills and mountains are readily formed from expanded polystyrene coated to prevent damage in use.

It is important to remember that once you have wargamed at a particular location, you are likely to wish to alter the battlefield terrain before the next game. For this reason, buildings must be portable and even the terrain moveable. For some, hills built up from flat pieces of expanded polystyrene, such as ceiling tiles, allow the soldiers to stand upright on the flat terraces of the hill. Modern vehicles, ships and aircraft are almost

Figure 13.23 Layouts for wargames not only employ plastics for buildings, trees and scatter materials but also for artillery, tanks and aircraft.

always assembled from plastic kits, often customised to suit the particular needs of the wargame, while, at the other extreme, you can hand make early siege engines from styrene sheet or casting resin, depending on the scale and number of items needed.

Military modelling

Military models are usually dioramas rather than complete landscapes. However, the creation of a diorama can be quite as demanding as a complete landscape and, just because it is smaller, tends to face more detailed and critical examination. A trench will not look right without the pile of earth in front of it; something that plastic scatter materials simulate realistically.

The amount of scenic materials you use will be considerably smaller than on a large layout, but the detail is usually much more impressive. Styrene sheet and strips are endlessly useful. Those representing corrugated iron are particularly useful for models representing scenes in the twentieth century.

Dioramas

A diorama is a scene or section of a scene usually used to display a particular model. It is often fitted in a custom-made perspex box. Dioramas are generally scratch-built, though a few kits do

Figure 13.24 On parade in front of their barracks, both the building and the figures offer the opportunity for the widespread use of plastics.

exist for displaying plastic models. The use of plastics in dioramas is widespread and you can treat them like small sections of a larger baseboard.

Making a diorama may be an end in itself, but often it is a means of displaying a particular model. Mostly, but by no means always incorporating figures, dioramas vary widely. Examples include:

- A hardened aircraft shelter housing the latest jet fighter.
- A ship at sea.

Figure 13.25 The motor cycle workshop shows off the use of a mixture of natural and man-made materials.

Figure 13.26
'Launching the lifeboat' is a stylish diorama which makes use of plastic materials for the men, animals and the sea itself.

- A model car being serviced in a garage.
- A locomotive on a length of railway line.
- A group of soldiers in battle.
- The crew inside a spaceship.
- A single room in a house.
- A shop front or interior.

Figures 13.25 and 13.26 show two exceptionally fine, but very different dioramas.

Chapter 14 Figures

Human figures come in all shapes, sizes and weights depending on their application. Some are made of thin silicone rubber, others of ABS, styrene or casting resin. Yet others, like dolls' house figures, may employ a mixture of plastics and natural materials.

Animal figures are usually made using the same materials and techniques as human figures though, on occasions, larger models are made from GRP. In addition, as mentioned in Chapter 6, the moulds for casting metal figures are frequently made from silicone rubber.

Ready-made plastic figures are simple to modify or adapt to a new role. You can alter the pose of figures made from thermoplastics by careful application of heat, while additional parts, such as helmet and goggles are readily formed from epoxy putty or styrene. However, you will need to choose an appropriate adhesive.

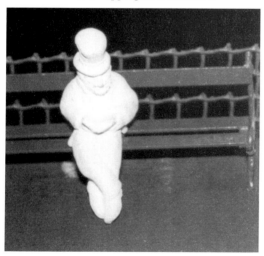

Figure 14.1 *This resin-cast figure is ready for painting.*

Aircraft pilots and crew

Nothing looks worse than a scale model of an aircraft such as a Spitfire without a pilot, or other crew as well if it is a Lancaster. For many people a head and shoulders figure suffices, but for the finest solution, a full-length figure is best. You can purchase vacuum-formed figures, usually in two halves ready for you to glue together, and these may be pre-painted by the manufacturer. Similar figures are available in silicone rubber, which has the advantage of being both light and flexible. Scales vary from 1/3rd to 1/12th or even

Figure 14.2 *A vacuum-formed jet pilot ready for installation. (Photo courtesy Vortex Plastics)*

121

Figure 14.3 A working model parachutist with control of his chute via the radio inside his torso.

smaller. You can equally well make your own using either technique.

Figure 14.3 shows a parachutist, made from plastic, with radio control built into the figure to enable you to steer the parachute from the ground when the model is dropped from a radio controlled model aircraft. You can readily construct such a model from GRP, making up the parachute from rip-stop nylon or terylene.

Animals

Making animals from kits of plastic parts is little different from making models of human beings. Casting animals, on the other hand, calls for a rather more complex mould and one is shown in Figure 6.11. Many models require figures on horseback, or even on camels, and a mix and match solution is often ideal for this. To make a farm, circus or zoo demands large numbers of animals. As a result, casting your own in resin can save large amounts of money.

Boat crew

In general, what suits an aircraft will also suit a working boat, although weight is much less of a

Figure 14.4 Building an animal from a set of plastic parts is relatively straightforward.

problem and, of course, the pose is likely to differ as is the dress. From Humphrey Bogart and Katherine Hepburn models in a steam-powered African Queen to naval officers and seamen on the admiral's barge, size, gender and clothing will vary.

Ready-made doll figures are usually plastic and, with judicious use of a heat gun, you can make them adopt a variety of poses. Man-made fabrics are much less affected by dampness or water and will dry out much more quickly if they accidentally get wet.

Dolls and puppets

Most dolls on the market, from Sindy to Action Man are made from tough plastic but the do-it-yourself field has made much less use of this material. You might think that plastics have no place in the construction of dolls, but it is surprising how useful these materials can be.

The head can be cast from plastic in a silicone rubber mould. The clothes may well make use of terylene or nylon and polyester thread is even more popular than cotton. While thin plastic fabrics have difficulty matching the flimsiness and flexibility of silk, they are certainly the next best thing.

For dolls' house figures, you can easily cast and paint your own dolls from polyester casting resin, providing a tough and durable finish.

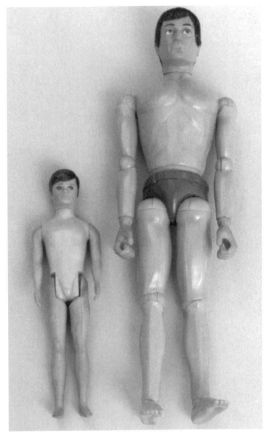

Figure 14.5 Action Man and smaller clones are ideal for customising and then dressing as the figure you require.

Figure 14.6 Making the sheer number of humans and animals in this circus calls for a vast amount of work.

Figure 14.8 This mould produces wonderful results as this doll's head shows. (Photo courtesy Alec Tiranti Ltd.)

plastics helps both in terms of weight and durability, particularly the ability to survive the inevitable bumps and knocks.

Figure 14.7 An elegant lady sits in a well-modelled horse-drawn vehicle.

Puppets are increasingly rare these days, yet there is a fascination in making and performing with them. The Spitting Image figures, used on British television, were made from synthetic rubber. Marionettes and rod puppets may be made in the same way as other figures and the use of

Figures for vehicles and trains

Whether you are looking for a driver for a radio controlled car or a farmer and his wife to fit in a horse-drawn cart, you can again use the same techniques as you would when making figures for any other working model. For smaller scales like slot-racing cars and model railways, adapting

Figure 14.9 There is plenty of scope for plastics when making puppets. These figures from **Sir Gawain and the Green Knight** *are operated by rods from the side.*

Figure 14.10 A silicone rubber mould and the metal-cast figure produced from it.

Figure 14.11 The figures bring this model of a Southdown bus station to life.

styrene figures or kits is one possibility while for a unique result, try making your own master and then cast the figure in a silicone rubber mould from low-melt metal or resin.

Military modelling

There are many military figures on the market in a variety of sizes, a majority made from styrene. Some are physically complete, just requiring painting, while others need full assembly, enabling you to customise the positions of the limbs and head. You can add specialist parts made from styrene sheet, rod or spare sprue to produce a completely individual character, while epoxy putty enables you to add a little padding here and there.

Such figures compete with metal-cast ones, which you can produce yourself if you are prepared to make both the initial master and a silicone rubber mould from it. The benefit is that many requirements call for large numbers of identical figures, which are easily produced once you have made the master mould. You can use the same technique for making resin-cast figures.

Wargaming figures

Serious wargaming is quite demanding from a modelling point of view. As well as large quantities

of figures for the armies, which may be ancient, medieval or modern, regular or guerrilla, infantry and cavalry, you will also need ancillary weapons and vehicles. These include tanks, armoured cars, artillery pieces, ballistas and siege towers, depending on the period depicted.

Figure 14.12 You can create wonderful mystical figures from styrene kits.

Figure 14.13
Most wargames
require signifi-
cant number of
model soldiers
to represent
the opposing
armies.

Figure 14.14 This 1/32nd injection-moulded fig-
ure has separate arms you attach to the torso.

Various scales are found in this hobby from 54mm – 1/32nd down to 6mm – 1/300th, the former representing the size of the original tin soldier while the latter better matches the size of the modern battlefield. It is not uncommon to find scales of 1/72nd, 1/76th, 1/87th and 20mm mixed together.

Ships from galleys to galleons, from aircraft carriers to battleships and not forgetting submarines are requisites for naval engagement. As mentioned in Chapter 9, the popularity of 1/72nd scale aircraft makes their provision for twentieth-century wargaming straightforward.

One of the easiest ways to make large numbers of figures is to cast them in low-melt metal in a silicone rubber mould. When casting, do not allow the mould to get too hot. Give it time to cool by itself every few casts and do not cool with water. Remember, however, that you are breaking copyright laws and effectively stealing, if you use a modern commercial figure as a master.

Polythene figures also have a major role but their flexibility tends to result in paint flaking off vulnerable areas such as spears and lances. Harder plastics like polystyrene are popular for wargaming as they overcome this difficulty. Figures made from this material usually need a degree of assembly. Plastic soldiers are widely available from both toy and model shops. In the smaller scales, it is common to find the soldiers grouped in blocks on a single base, usually cut from styrene sheet.

Converting figures

Plastic figures are much easier to convert to a different pose or alter to give a particular distinctive look than metal ones. Use a sharp craft knife and try to make clean cuts rather than using a sawing action which will leave ragged edges.

Because plastic figures are made from thermoplastics, you can use heat to reshape them. Immersion in hot water may suffice to soften the figure enough to bend it into a new pose. An alternative is a hot-air gun to soften the figure and a hot needle stuck through a cork, or a heated knife blade, which you can use to seal joints.

You can give figures new heads, or even cut them in half at the waist and mix and match different tops and bottoms. Gluing is sometimes difficult with polythene, though polystyrene is straightforward, but Chapter 4 gives some good advice on suitable adhesives. Furthermore, you can support a vulnerable point like the neck with an embedded length of pin or thin piano wire, when a head has been replaced.

Before painting plastic figures, remove any grease remaining on them from the moulding process with soapy water and then thoroughly dry them.

Chapter 15 Model engineering

The hobby of model engineering is based on the working of metals to produce tools and complete models. Material lists include a vast range of pure and alloyed metals. It is not an area that has traditionally been associated with the use of plastics, although the application of these materials is increasingly common. The so-called engineering plastics include acetal, nylon, polycarbonate and PTFE.

Most lathes use plastic belts for connecting the motor to the head stock and the Unimat 1, which many would hardly consider a genuine machine tool, is a miniature lathe and milling machine made almost entirely from plastic. You will also find plastics widely used as file handles, to provide soft heads for hammers and even as soft vice jaws.

A search of any of the good model engineering catalogues will reveal a choice of plastics on offer; adhesives like the range of Loctite and Araldite products, O-rings, seals, belt drives and flexible pipe work are areas where plastics are making their mark. Post steam-era locomotive bodies are often made from GRP while PTFE bearings and epoxy putties are increasingly popular.

Before looking at the potential of plastics in the individual branches of model engineering, it is useful to examine the various plastic components and materials on the market.

Bearings

While traditionally bearings have always been made from metal, the use of plastics for these purposes is increasing. Materials like nylon and PTFE are easy to machine, are hard wearing and mostly self-lubricating. They thus provide a virtually maintenance-free solution to many bearing requirements. They are easily machined and drilled to size. There is information about the potential dangers of overheating PTFE, when machining it, on page 32.

Belt drives

Belt drives are as old as engineering itself, but the replacement of flat leather belts with a wide

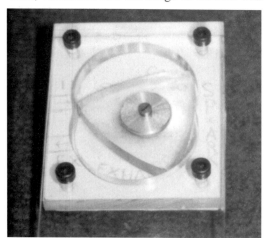

Figure 15.1 *An unusual use of perspex to show the internal workings of a Wankel engine.*

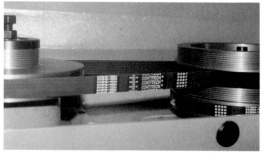

Figure 15.2 *A typical poly-V plastic drive belt on a pillar drill.*

Figure 15.3 A flat belt drive takes power from this loco-motive style steam engine.

range of plastics belts of a variety of shapes has transformed power transmission. Gear and chain drives can easily be simplified and made more reliable by the substitution of plastic belts.

Toothed belts

Typical toothed belts come in a range of sizes and lengths and are 98% efficient at transmitting power at speed of up to 80 m/s. Depending on their construction, they will operate over a relatively wide temperature range.

They will run quietly without maintenance or slip and provide a positive drive where you need accurate position or timing. These belts can run on steel or moulded glass-filled polycarbonate toothed wheels.

Poly-V belts, round belts and V or wedge belts

Synthetic rubber is the basis for all of these drive belts, though they are usually manufactured with specially treated sheathings to help with anti-static, oil and fire resistance. As a temporary measure, you can cut them to size and join them with cyano adhesive. You can permanently join some of them with a hot knife.

Twist-link belting

This type of belt, made from reinforced polyester fabric, features low stretch, drive tension and

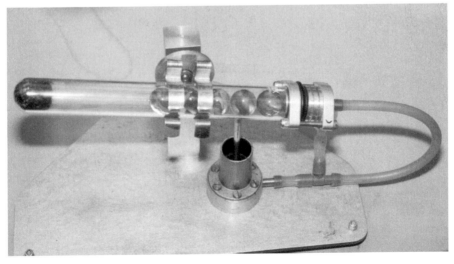

Figure 15.4 This hot-air 'engine' has a nylon T-piece, and uses a silicone rubber seal and tubing.

Figure 15.5 A set of plastic change wheels from a Hobbymat lathe.

vibration. You can easily make a belt to any length and this type is perfect as an emergency replacement belt when something breaks in the workshop just after the shops have closed.

Diaphragms

Sheet neoprene is relatively impermeable to gases and is readily cut to the size and shape needed for making diaphragms. It is also useful for making flexible gaskets as it is one of the stronger synthetic rubbers.

Electroplating

Polythene and polypropylene containers, such as those which contain ice cream in bulk, make ideal tanks for holding the electrolyte and any pre-treatment solutions. You can even electroplate

Figure 15.6 Plastic gears are sometimes useful for steam engine auxiliary drives.

some plastics, such as resin-cast figures, by first coating them with a conductive metal-loaded paint.

Flexible pipes

Flexible pipes have many applications in model engineering from air compressor connections to steam, gas and lubrication piping. Silicone rubber tube resists heat well, but is fairly soft and vulnerable in harsh environments. It is also attacked by petrol and diesel fuels. Neoprene and clear plastic tube, on the other hand, are impervious to attack by these liquids. Reinforced plastic piping is ideal for compressed air leads. Pumping suds is a particular need and plug-together commercial systems use acetal components to build up pipe work.

Friction rollers

Often, a plain friction drive is sufficient to move a part, such as a model conveyor belt. You can stick synthetic sheet rubber to your own metal roller with cyano or contact adhesive. Alternatively you can buy synthetic rubber rollers or salvage them from old photocopying machines and printers.

Gears

Plastic worms and wheels are a satisfactory alternative to phosphor bronze running against steel when machined from delrin and can be run against each other. Alternatively you can use a delrin wheel with a steel worm, which will transmit more than twice the torque.

You can make spur or helical gears from delrin or tufnol and, in terms of power transmission, they have roughly the same performance as brass gears of a similar size. Most plastic gears are available from suppliers in ready-machined form and many spur gears are cheaply available in moulded form as are racks.

A range of lubricants suitable for plastic-to-plastic and metal-to-plastic gears includes the following greases:

Castrol Alpha gel and Spheerol AP1
Mobil Glygol 00
Shell Alvania R1 and Tivella comp A

Figure 15.7 You can even tap into your repair if you use Roket Powder with cyano to make good the error. (Photo courtesy Deluxe Materials)

Heat-insulation materials

While the main use of heat-insulation materials is likely to be for boilers and steam pipes, there is often a need to insulate a workshop itself. The use of asbestos is totally unacceptable but plastic-derived substitutes allow you to lag boilers and steam pipes, while expanded polystyrene is one of the most popular choices for insulating workshop buildings.

Seals and O-rings

Loctite 542 works as an excellent steam-proof gasket for cylinders and steam chests. Nitrile rubber or viton O-rings and nitrile-rubber cord, joined with a suitably matching grade of cyano glue, and V-ring seals, are useful at each end of gauge glasses on steam generators. Gland packings made from pure PTFE, PTFE/graphited GFO fibre or kevlar/aramid fibre all withstand high pressures, reasonable temperatures and rotation speeds. PTFE tape is ideal for sealing low pressure water pipes.

You can make your own silicone rubber seals by turning a mould in the lathe from hard, blue machining wax and then pouring catalysed silicone rubber into the mould and leaving it to cure.

Shims

You can use sheets of plastic shim, colour coded in thickness from 0.05mm – 0.5mm for the same jobs as metal shim. The thinner sheets are of polyester and the thicker ones from polypropylene. You can also use these materials as a barrier to prevent corrosion between dissimilar metals.

Shock and vibration mounts

The most popular use of these mounts, almost invariably made from synthetic rubber, is in the

Table 15.1 The performance of some gland packing materials.

Material	Pressure	Max temperature	Rotation speed
Pure PTFE	200 bar	280°C	7 m/s
PTFE/graphited GFO fibre	200 bar	280°C	10 m/s
Kevlar/aramid fibre	400 bar	280°C	15 m/s

mounting of small internal-combustion engines in model aircraft, boats, cars, lorries and loco-motives. Single-cylinder engines are renowned for the level of vibration they produce and four-stroke engines are worse in this respect than two-stroke ones.

Tippex

This correcting fluid is also ideal for coating metal surfaces which you do not wish to get covered with silver solder or spelter when brazing. It is easily painted on with the brush included in each pot and removed afterwards with its own thinners. Tippex is basically a suspension of white solid in trichlorethan.

Figure 15.8 *This electric clock is mounted on plastic insulators and has a perspex clock face.*

Tufnol leaf springs

Laminated tufnol strip is useful for making leaf springs both for road and railway vehicles and is sold in a range of sizes for this purpose from 9mm x 0.8mm to 19mm x 1.5mm in 1220mm lengths. It has the two advantages in that it deflects under lighter loads than the steel equivalent and, of course, it never rusts.

Applications

Model engineering has many branches, so that particular disciplines will make varying uses of plastics.

Clocks

You may question whether a clock is a model, as almost all are built to a scale of 1:1. Moreover, for many, the thought of ruining a beautiful brass clock with any plastic parts is unthinkable, yet for others the wide availability of plastic items such as clock hands and numerals proves irre-sistible. If you are trying to simulate ivory, plastic is today the only legal solution. Plastic domes are available to cover clocks and are much less prone to accidental breakage than glass.

Electric-powered clocks, often dating back to the early part of the twentieth century, make more extensive use of plastic materials, particularly in

Figure 15.9 *The original ivory hands and figures of this clock were replaced with plastic ones.*

Figure 15.10 A small petrol aero-engine with a plastic tank and ignition components.

Figure 15.11 An engine with its home-made silencer sealed to its exhaust stub with Hemetite.

the form of insulators and Figure 15.8 shows that even acrylic has a place in clock building, here used to provide the clock face. You may also wish to consider PTFE as a low-friction, lubrication-free bearing material.

Internal-combustion engines

There are two areas where model engines benefit from plastics. The first is in making fuel tanks, where the transparency of plastic allows you to see how much fuel remains, and the second is when connecting the tank to the carburretor. Take care to select a plastic which is not attacked by your fuel. The second area is in the insulation of various parts of the ignition system on petrol engines. Both can be seen in Figure 15.10.

Model guns

It is normal for models of guns to be fabricated entirely from metal and wood, following full-size practice. The question that then arises is whether there is ever a case for employing plastics.

Probably the most important area is the tyres for guns of Second World War and later vintage. These are readily moulded in blackened silicone rubber, or you can base the whole size of model on the availability of suitable synthetic rubber tyres.

Figure 15.12 It is relatively straightfor-ward to make synthetic rub-ber tyres for a model like this magnificent twenty-five pounder artil-lery piece.

Here, however, we are more concerned with using plastics to protect or repair machine tools, or in the building of accessories for them.

Chapter 3 has already indicated how best to sharpen tools for working plastics when drilling, turning or milling them. Sheet plastic covers are ideal for protection of tools in any workshop where condensation is not a problem. You can make your own plastic bearings, particularly where low friction and self-lubrication are important. You can also use plastics for insulation in tools like band saw-blade welders and in the control systems for electrically powered items.

Scientific instruments

Scientific instrument reproduction often involves parts which, in the prototype, were made from ivory. It is now illegal to import this natural material into the UK and many other countries, which leaves little alternative but to search for a realistic plastic alternative. Styrene or ABS sheet are probably the best substitutes and both are readily engraved.

The insides of boxes are easily covered with self-adhesive plastic baize, readily available in the green favoured by instrument makers. Red is also popular but other colours are harder to find.

Steam-powered models

Tyres for traction engines are better made from synthetic rubber than the real thing and it is not

Figure 15.13 Synthetic rubber tyres are relatively cheap, long lasting and oil resistant.

Machine and other workshop tools

Machine tools not only make increasing use of plastics but, as already mentioned, some like the Unimat 1 are made almost entirely of plastic.

Figure 15.14 A band saw-blade welder with significant chunks of plastic insulation material.

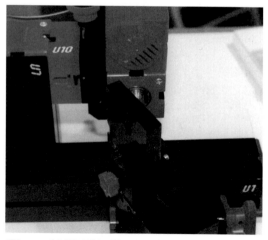

Figure 15.15 This Unimat 1 is set up to mill a piece of coloured acrylic.

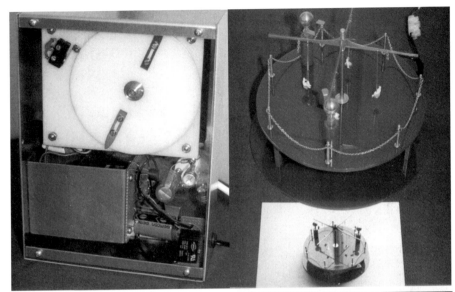

Figure 15.16 The driver, left and the electrostatically powered roundabout both make plenty of use of plastics in their basic construction.

unusual to find plastic seats or seat coverings. In the same way, flexible plastic water pipes can simulate the rubber ones used on the prototype. Lagging is always a concern on models with boilers, particularly those fitted with a painted metal cladding. A material like Klingersil, although relatively expensive, is an excellent alternative to asbestos.

Other vehicles

Lorries will need rubber tyres and synthetic rubber is generally recommended for this purpose. The leather upholstery for the driver's and other seats of any passenger-carrying vehicle is easily simulated from vinyl cloth. Windscreens, side and rear windows should not be made from plate glass for safety reasons. You can use clear acetate, butyrate or perspex sheet as a substitute, depending on the size of the model, and the same also applies for the light fittings.

Hot-air engines

Perhaps more than in any other area of model engineering, Stirling engines benefit from the use of plastics. You can make displacers from expanded polystyrene, the more dense varieties lasting longer, while cylinders and other parts are readily produced from acrylic or even underground grade, large-diameter gas pipe. Diaphragm engines almost always employ airtight neoprene

Figure 15.17 A typical hot-air engine. This one has an acrylic flywheel and polystyrene displacer.

for this critical part. Whatever plastics you choose, be sure that they are not so close to the hot end of the machine that you damage or melt them.

PTFE bearings result in remarkably low levels of frictional loss and have the added advantage of not requiring lubrication.

Plastic engineering

Quite a few people build models from unexpected materials. Examples include large-scale locomotives

and traction engines built from plastic card and wood rather than from metal.

If they are powered, it is usually by an electric motor rather than steam. Plastic boxes and tubes with the addition of custom parts cut from styrene sheet can result in a model which replicates the prototype in almost every area except its power source.

The speed of construction using plastics is, of course, much faster and normally you only need hand tools for working these basic materials. You will, however, need to make a careful selection of suitable adhesives following the advice given in Chapter 4. The end result, once carefully painted, is often indistinguishable from a model made from metal, apart from the weight!

Chapter 16 Electrical and electronics

Modern electronics would never have developed as far and as rapidly as it has, had it not been for matching developments in plastic materials. You may not, on the whole, need to know or care how plastics are used in the manufacturing side of electronics, but materials for making and housing printed circuit boards are another matter.

By their very nature as excellent insulators, plastics also tend to build up high levels of static charge. This can be a lethal problem for some electronic components such as CMOS integrated circuits.

Fortunately, there is a range of anti-static products to help solve these problems. For electronics, carbon-loaded polypropylene or co-polymer styrene, both of which are black and conductive, are widely used for storage containers. For bags, mats and working surfaces, a dissipative plastic material, usually a form of PVC with a buried metallic layer, is a common solution

For repairing any damaged tracks on printed circuit boards, silver-loaded epoxy adhesives provide both the required strength and electrical conductivity.

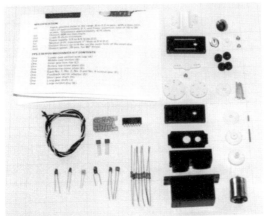

Figure 16.1 There are endless plastics used in both the electronic and mechanical parts of this kit for a radio controlled servo. Materials include GRP, nylon, polycarbonate, polypropylene, PVC, and synthetic rubber.

Figure 16.2 Typical of the use of plastics in electronics, this fail safe for a radio controlled submarine uses a home-etched GRP circuit board housed in a plastic box, protected with plastic foam.

Capacitors

Many capacitors are classed by the plastic used in their construction and the particular plastic will affect some of the main characteristics of the capacitor.

Thus electronic component catalogues will list polycarbonate, polyester (mylar), polypropylene and polystyrene capacitors, reflecting the insulation used between their plates. These and other types may be resin dipped and/or epoxy sealed.

Polypropylene – A low-loss dielectric suitable for high voltages and fast rise-time pulses.

Polycarbonate – Provides high stability and linear temperature effects.

Polyester (mylar) – Ideal for coupling and decoupling applications.

Polystyrene – Gives a high insulation resistance but lower operating temperature range than polycarbonate or polyester types.

Resin dipping and epoxy sealing both help to protect the complete component from its environment. Sometimes glass fibre-reinforced, flame resistant cases, which are sealed with epoxy resin, are used in automobile applications.

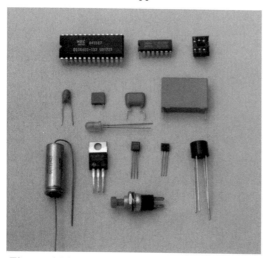

Figure 16.3 Many electronic components, particularly integrated circuits, are enclosed in one or other plastic material for insulation and environmental protection.

Conduit and trunking

When building, for example, a new workshop in a wooden shed, plastic conduit and trunking to house the electric cables is the first choice for many people and is available in a range of sizes and shapes.

Most popular is the oval-section conduit which is embedded in the wall plaster during building construction. However, you can also obtain circular, square and rectangular shapes together with joints, terminal boxes, elbows, bends and tees. Almost all are made from PVC and a solvent-weld adhesive is usually recommended by the manufacturer for making joints.

Containers and housings

The range of boxes of various shapes and sizes available from companies like Maplin and Electromail is enormous, and many make special provision in their moulding for locating printed circuit boards and transformers. Typical materials used are high-impact polystyrene, often flame-resistant, high impact ABS, polycarbonate which is usually flame retardant and used where the hinge is in-built, or self-extinguishing glass-reinforced polyester.

Insulators and seals

Plastics are, by their very nature, excellent insulators. Sheet, strip, foam and tape are all able to provide isolation and protection for delicate electronics. You can use synthetic rubber strip or silicone rubber to seal containers, housings and cable entry and exit points.

Heat-shrink tube

Heat-shrink tubing made from irradiated polyolefin will shrink to less than half its supplied diameter when heated to a temperature between 120°C and 200°C.

Heat-shrink tube is designed to support soldered wire connections to plugs and sockets. It is also ideal for covering made-up battery packs and holding them securely together.

Both clear and coloured variants are produced. The latter, though normally black, typically comes in six different colours including green/yellow stripe for earth leads. A variant made from modified polyvinylidene fluoride will withstand higher temperatures (up to 175°C) than the standard variant which is only rated up to 135°C.

Heat-sink compounds

These pastes are normally made from a metal oxide in a silicone base and are ideal for use when bolting components to heat sinks. You can also bond heat sinks in place with a fast-curing acrylic adhesive which has excellent thermal transfer characteristics.

Nuts, bolts and spacers

When mounting a printed circuit in a metal box, it is important to insulate it from its housing. Plastic nuts and bolts, usually made from nylon, are ideal for this purpose and are amazingly strong.

Small nylon spacers are often essential both mechanically and to provide insulation when mounting completed printed circuit boards in metal cases or completed models

PCBs (printed circuit boards)

There are two commonly used plastics for printed circuit boards; GRP, commonly called fibreglass

Figure 16.4 Printed circuit boards are normally made from paxolin or GRP laminate. Strip board is usually paxolin-based.

and paxolin. The former is much stronger and also more expensive, but is the first choice for mobile and other applications which demand a degree of ruggedness. Paxolin board is somewhat

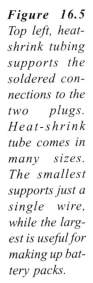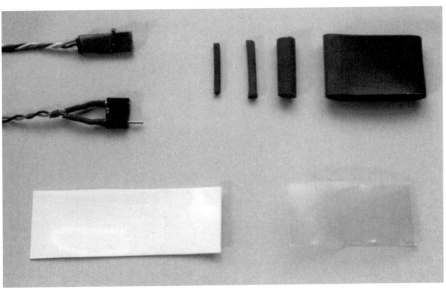

Figure 16.5 Top left, heat-shrink tubing supports the soldered connections to the two plugs. Heat-shrink tube comes in many sizes. The smallest supports just a single wire, while the largest is useful for making up battery packs.

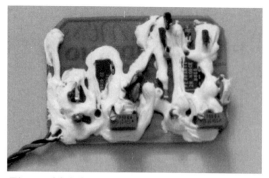

Figure 16.6 Components supported by a liberal application of silicone rubber.

thicker to provide the necessary rigidity. Both materials are easily drilled, but GRP will rapidly blunt even a high speed steel drill.

Wiring

All wiring these days is insulated with plastic. Normal equipment hook-up wire and household electrical cables are covered with PVC. Coaxial cable has a polythene insulator between the conductor and the braiding. Coated solid copper wire, usually self-fluxing and used for winding cores and transformers is covered with a thin layer of polyurethane varnish.

For the best flexibility and high temperature resistance, silicone rubber-covered leads are the ideal solution. For hot and chemically adverse environments, high-temperature wires and cables which are PTFE insulated, with or without a covering of glass mica tape, are a good solution. Silicone rubber insulation with an aluminium laminate and LSOH goes even further in terms of being fire resistant.

Potting

For high physically stressed applications, such as a transistorised ignition unit for an internal combustion engine, it is essential to support each

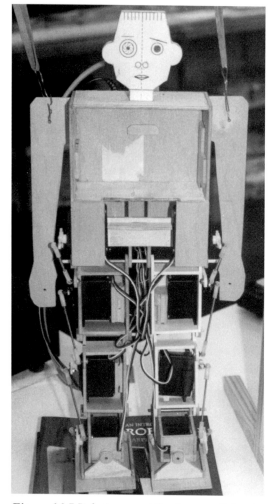

Figure 16.7 Robots cry out for the use of plastics for their bodies.

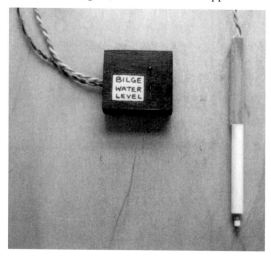

Figure 16.8 This home-made water sensor uses concentric styrene rods for insulation and a small electronic amplifier potted in epoxy.

individual component from the ravages of vibration. This is classically achieved by putting the circuit in a container and then filling it with epoxy resin. A satisfactory alternative, where the container is sealed, is to use silicone rubber to provide the support.

Robotics

Harprit Sandhu's excellent book, *An Introduction to Robotics* (Nexus Special Interests), describes creating a walking robot with the body built largely from plywood. This is an interesting approach, but the use of plastics would allow the construction of a more realistic and probably lighter weight robot. The realism arises from the ability to form curves from thermoplastics, or to mould three-dimensional parts from GRP. Shaping the head, hands and feet from GRP would also be quite simple.

An alternative and more off-beat approach is to make models of robots partly or entirely from perspex so that the interior construction is visible.

Appendix A Bibliography and list of useful addresses

Bibliography

Adhesives Handbook John Shields (Butterworth & Co (Publishers) Ltd 1984)
Adhesives and Sealants David Lammas (Nexus Special Interests 1991)
Cold Cure Silicone Rubber for Mould Making (Alec Tiranti Ltd 1990)
Creative Plastics Techniques Claude Smale (Van Nostrand Reinhold 1973)
Do it yourself Vacuum Forming Douglas E Walsh (Vacuum Form 1990)
The Glassfibre Handbook R.H.Warring (Nexus Special Interests 1989)
Moulding and Glassfibre Techniques Peter Holland (Nexus Special Interests 1989)
Plastics John Brydson (Science Museum 1991)
Plastics Craftwork and Technology D P Greenwood (John Murray 1980)
Plastics Materials J A Brydson (Chemical Publishing Co. Inc. 1979)
Plastic Structure Kits Iain Rice. (Wild Swan Publications Ltd. 1988)
Polymer Technology D R Miles and J H Briston (Illife Books Ltd. 1996)
The Polyester Resin Booklet. (Alec Tiranti Ltd 1990)
Radio Control Foam Modelling David Thomas (Nexus Special Interests 1989)
The Strand Guide to Fibreglass (Scott Bader Co. Ltd. 1988)
Styrene Handbook (Evergreen Scale Models Inc.)
Wills Scenic Series Catalogue and Handbook (Wills Kits)

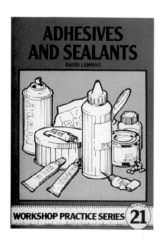
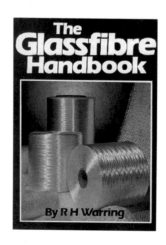
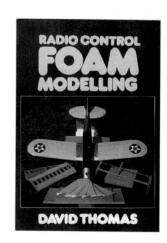

List of useful addresses

British Plastics Foundation,
6, Bath Place,
Rivington St.,
London, EC2A 3JE.

Deluxe Materials, – Stockist: Irvine Engines
Thornton House,
Soke Rd., Silchester,
Reading, Berks, RG7 2NS.

The Dolls House Emporium
Victoria Rd.,
Ripley,
Derbyshire, DE5 3YD.

Electromail,
PO Box 99,
Corby,
Nothants, NN17 9RS.

Evergreen Scale Models, Inc.
12808 N.E. 125th Way,
Kirkland,
WA 98034, USA

Frost Restoration Techniques Ltd.
Crawford St.,
Rochdale,
Lancs. OL16 5NU.

W. Hobby Ltd.,
Knight's Hill Sq.,
London,
SE27 0HH.

Humbrol Ltd., – Owners of Airfix
Marfleet,
Hull,
North Humberside, HU9 5NE.

Irvine Ltd.,
Unit 2, Brunswick Ind. Park,
Brunswick Way, New Southgate,
London, N11 1JL.

Maplin MPS,
PO Box 777,
Rayleigh,
Essex, SS6 8LU.

Minicraft Macford Products Ltd.,
1&2, Enterprise City,
Meadowfield Avenue,
Spennymoor, Co Durham, DL16 6JF.

Nexus Special Interests,
Nexus House, Azalea Drive,
Swanley,
Kent, BR8 8HU.

Ratio Plastic Models,
Hamlyn House, Mardle Way,
Buckfastleigh,
Devon, TQ11 0NS.

Revell GB Ltd.,
Foster House, Maxwell Rd.
Borehamwood,
Herts., WD6 1JB.

Slaters Plastikard Ltd.,
Temple Rd.,
Matlock Bath,
Derbyshire.

Strand Retail,
Scott Bader Co. Ltd.
Wollaston, Wellingborough,
Northants., NN9 7RL.

Vortex Plastics,
73, Sonehill Avenue,
Birstall,
Leicester, LE4 4JF.

Wills Kits,
Lower Road,
Forrest Row,
Sussex RH18 5HE.

Index of plastics

ABS (acrylonitrile butadiene styrene)	2
Acetal (polyacetal)	2
Acetate	4
Acrylic (polymethyl methacrylate)	3,11
Aminos	12
Bakelite	12
Butyrate	4
CAB (cellulose acetate butyrate)	4
Cab-O-Sil	16
Casein	xvi
Cast nylon 6	5
Catalysts for silicone rubber	16
Celluloid	4
Cellulose acetate	4
Cellulose nitrate	4
Cellulose plastics	4
Chloroprene rubber	17
Composites	64
Corex and cocotherm	7
Dacron	7
Delrin	3
Diene rubber	16
DP.100	16
Duracon	3
Epoxy	11, 47 66
Expanded polystyrene	9, 73
Fablon	11
Fluon	9
Formaldehydes (aminos)	12
Formica	13
Glass filled nylon 66	5
GRP	64
Hot-melt vinyl	10, 62
Isopon	14
Kevlar	5, 68
Klingersil	16
Latex	62
Lexan	7
Maestro acrylic/PVA polymers	16
Melamine	13
Melinex	7
MF (melamine formaldehyde)	13
MoS^2 filled cast nylon 6	5
Mylar	7
Neoprene	17
Nylatron GS	5
Nyloil	5
Nylon	4
Nylon 66	5
Olefin rubber	16
Paxolin	12
Perspex	4
Phenol formaldehyde (PF)	12
Phenolics	12
Phenolic laminates	12
Plasticard	8, 82
Plastruct	8, 82
Polyamides	4
Polycarbonate	6
Polyester	7, 14, 48, 66
Polyethylene	7
Polypropylene	8
Polystyrene	8
Polythene	7
Polyurethane	14, 77
PTFE (polytetrafluoroethylene)	9
PVA (polyvinyl acetate)	9, 48
PVC (polyvinyl chloride)	11
Resin casting	70
RTV-11, RTV-31, RTV-420, RTV-428	15
SF-96-50 silicone fluid	15
Silicone rubber	15, 57
Styrene	8, 79
Synthetic rubber	16
Teflon	9
Terylene	7
Tixo TA1 thixotropic additive	15
Torlon	6
Tufnol	6
Tufset	15
UF (urea formaldehyde)	13, 49
Victrex	14
Vinyl	10
Viton	9